Advanced Marker Techniques

Advanced Marker Techniques

Dick Powell and Patricia Monahan

Macdonald Orbis

A Macdonald Orbis book

© Macdonald & Co Publishers Ltd. 1987
© Text Dick Powell 1987

First published in Great Britain in 1987 by
Macdonald & Co (Publishers) Ltd
London & Sydney

Reprinted 1989

A member of Maxwell Pergamon
Publishing Corporation plc

British Library Cataloguing in Publication Data

Powell, Dick
   Marker techniques.
   1. Commercial art   2. Felt marker
   drawing
   I. Title   II. Monahan, Patricia
   741.6   NC997

   ISBN 0-356-14279-5

Macdonald & Co (Publishers) Ltd
66-73 Shoe Lane
London
EC4P 4AB

Colour reproduction by Colorlito

Printed in Italy
ISBN: 0-356-14279-5

Designer: Mike Wade

Contents

Introduction

The origins of the humble marker go back a long way; indeed the first markers, made from bamboo and a felt nib, originated in Japan many years ago. The first commercial marker, however, was not launched until the mid sixties. It was blotchy and unpredictable, but offered two advantages that no other media of that era could match – a fast drying time, and convenience.

Design Studio: Philips C.I.D, Eindhoven

This rendering of a radio design is typical of the output of industrial design studios. It is drawn in side elevation so that dimensional accuracy and scale can be maintained, and the detail on which such a drawing depends can be quickly put in using rulers, circle guides and so on. Many different media, such as pastels and crayons, have been used over the basic marker work to achieve more subtle modelling of the forms and details, and gouache has been used for the final highlights.

Back in the sixties, the idea of manufacturing 150 different colours, each in its own small 6cc bottle which would stand only a few minutes of continuous use, seemed utterly ridiculous when compared to a palette of gouache. Now of course, there are hundreds of different brands, colours and types of marker for working on different surfaces and for producing different effects. The basic advantages remain: the main one is the fast drying time that allows the user to overlay colours immediately, without the intermixing common to other media (such as paint), so that full-colour visuals can be produced without the need for extensive preparation. Another benefit of markers is that they work best on lightweight semi-transparent papers which allow extensive use of underlays, so that paper stretching and tracing down are unnecessary. Markers have a third plus factor: familiarity with a particular brand gives the artist a colour memory that makes selection and use quick and easy. For these reasons the marker has come to dominate much of the graphics business, completely surplanting traditional media for many applications. When it first arrived, however, it

demanded a new approach, and so artists and designers had to alter their styles and develop new techniques to take full advantage of it. These were hard-won skills, and for anyone, student or professional, who is inexperienced with markers, it is a daunting task to acquire them by trial and error and it can take a long time. This book will not help you to draw, and it will not turn you into an accomplished marker artist, but, by showing some of the basic techniques and tricks of the trade alongside fine examples of marker renderings, it can help you move up that learning curve a bit faster.

Drawing is absolutely fundamental to marker rendering (or any kind of visualizing for that matter), and without this skill the marker is as limited as any other colouring media. This book assumes that you can draw reasonably well and that you are used to drawing from life, from memory, or from reference material. From such a base it will help the beginner acquire marker rendering skills, and it should offer the more experienced a useful insight into how others achieve different finishes and effects. The book starts with a guide to the most common materials used by the marker artist. This is followed by two chapters that are devoted to practical stage-by-stage examples showing how drawings are created, and which include favoured techniques developed by individual artists and designers. The remaining eight chapters are devoted to specific applications. Each of these chapters gives numerous examples of drawings, from roughs and scamps through to finished artwork and illustrations, with a description of how they were done. These examples can be analysed for their technique and learned from, but more importantly, they are a source of inspiration, both for the beginner and for the experienced professional.

Artist: Paul Langford

This punchy image (right), is deliberately simplified so that the idea can be put across to the client quickly and efficiently. The artist has used the marker with absolute confidence and it shows! This boldness of approach is vital for producing slick, but informative, loose visuals.

Design Studio: The Design House
Artist: Nigel Langford

A nice loose visual (below), with a fluid sketchy feel to it. The designer has obtained a good impression of the interior with the minimum of marks on the paper; note especially how the white of the paper is allowed to show through so that the drawing looks fresh rather than overworked.

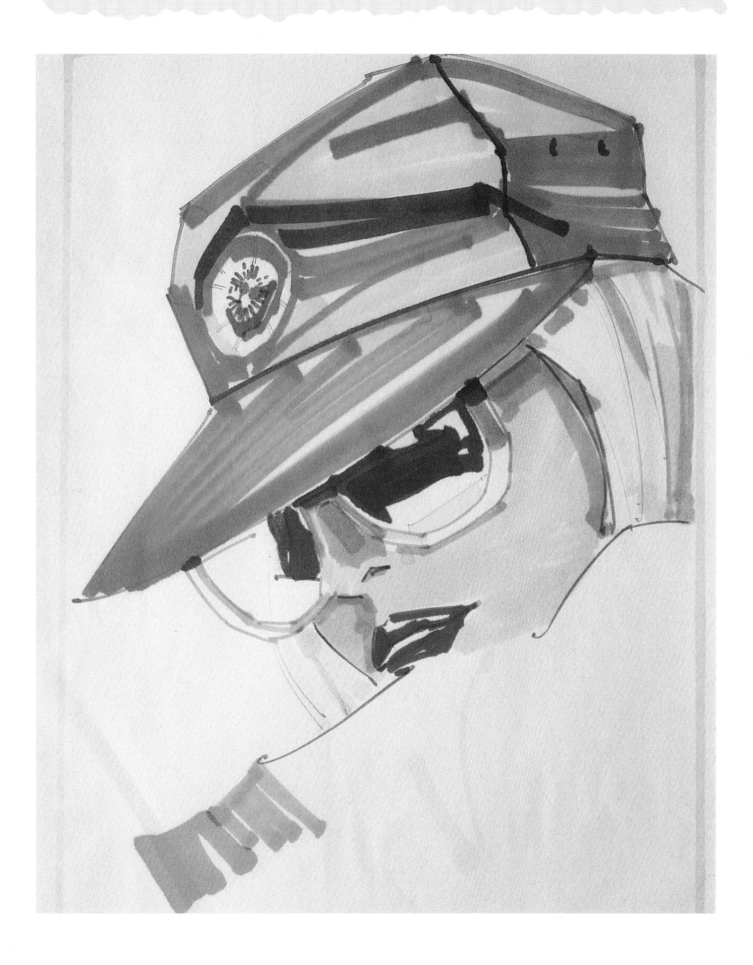

1 Materials

There is a bewildering choice of markers available and every artist has a preference for a particular product. Having established that one works well and suits his or her particular style, the artist will stay with it and avoid alternative brands which might introduce a new, unforeseen effect at the wrong moment. Seasoned artists need no advice on what to use, but for the newcomer it is often difficult to know what to buy. It may seem obvious to say so, but do buy the best available and learn how to look after your materials. What follows is a personal appraisal of currently available materials, how they work and what to look out for.

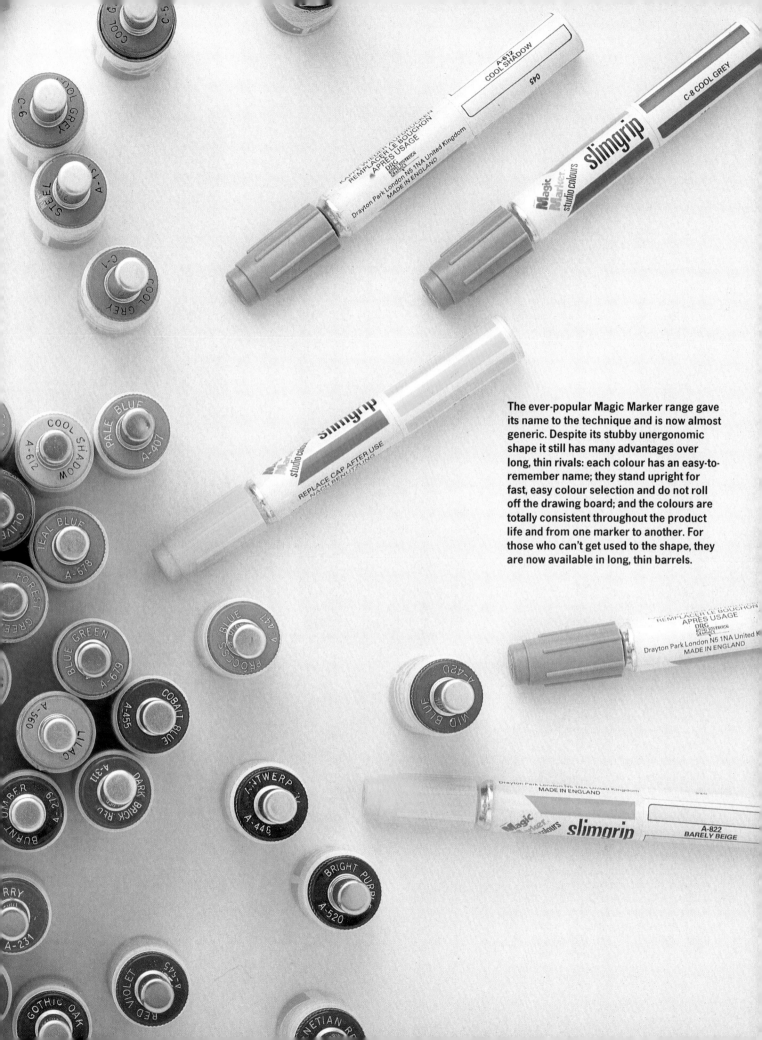

The ever-popular Magic Marker range gave its name to the technique and is now almost generic. Despite its stubby unergonomic shape it still has many advantages over long, thin rivals: each colour has an easy-to-remember name; they stand upright for fast, easy colour selection and do not roll off the drawing board; and the colours are totally consistent throughout the product life and from one marker to another. For those who can't get used to the shape, they are now available in long, thin barrels.

Marker range and tonal rendering

One important secret of good rendering is knowing how to use colour effectively to model three-dimensional objects. The world is a three-dimensional place, and virtually everything you want to depict has form which reflects light and throws shadows. Sometimes you may be working with hard objects with clearly defined breaks in the form; in such cases, sharp contrast between surfaces won't look odd and is often desirable. And at other times you will be dealing with soft organic surfaces which blend and flow together in smooth tonal transitions. In the former case it doesn't matter if the colour dries before you apply an adjacent shade, but in the latter you need to work fast to keep the colour wet so that newly laid colours can be subtly blended. In either case the real trick is recognizing which colours work well together to give sufficient tonal contrast, and yet can be successfully blended for tonal transitions. This usually comes with practice and experience, but for the beginner investing in markers for the first time a chart, such as the one shown right, can save a lot of time testing markers in the shop, and a lot of money buying unnecessary colours. If you are new to marker rendering it is always a good idea to keep a reference chart such as this so that you have a record of what works and what doesn't. If you do make a chart, be sure to use your regular marker paper and fix it to a board with a tape hinge down the centre; this will allow you to fold over the paper and thus protect the colours from direct light.

The standard method of creating two tones of the same colour is through overlaying: the colour is laid down once, allowed to dry, and then overlaid again. This gives quite a subtle tonal shift which is usually insufficient for sharp modelling so a second, darker colour is needed. The beginner is often tempted to use cool or warm greys for this shadow tone, but this invariably makes the colour 'muddy'. To keep the perception of the colour clear and bright it is essential to choose a new colour. This second colour can, in turn, be overlaid to produce a still darker tone. A third colour is usually necessary to produce the really dark tones, and this can also be overlaid yet again for the deep shadows. In this way, a subtle transition of six tones can be produced by careful selection and overlaying.

The colour chart right was rendered with the Magic Marker range, but it could easily be carried out in any other brand, although some experimentation would be needed. The limitations of printing have made it very difficult to achieve accurate colour matchings, so you should only refer to the colour names when referring to this chart. Each colour has been used only once (unless stated as overlaid x2) to give a reasonable tonal balance, but more subtle effects can be obtained through overlaying.

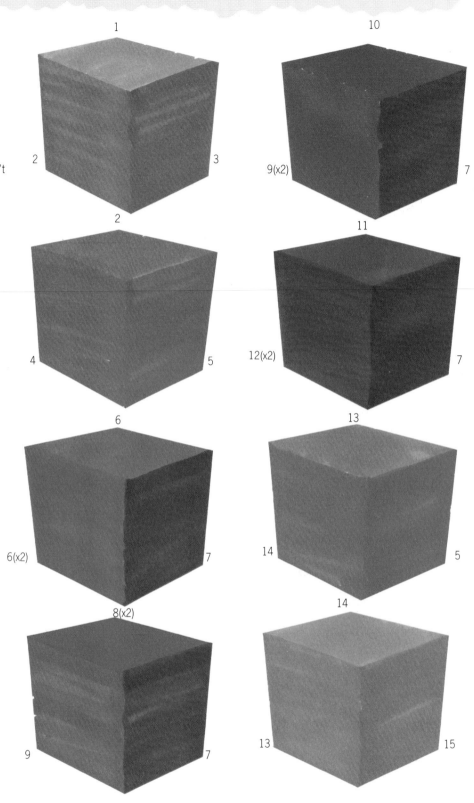

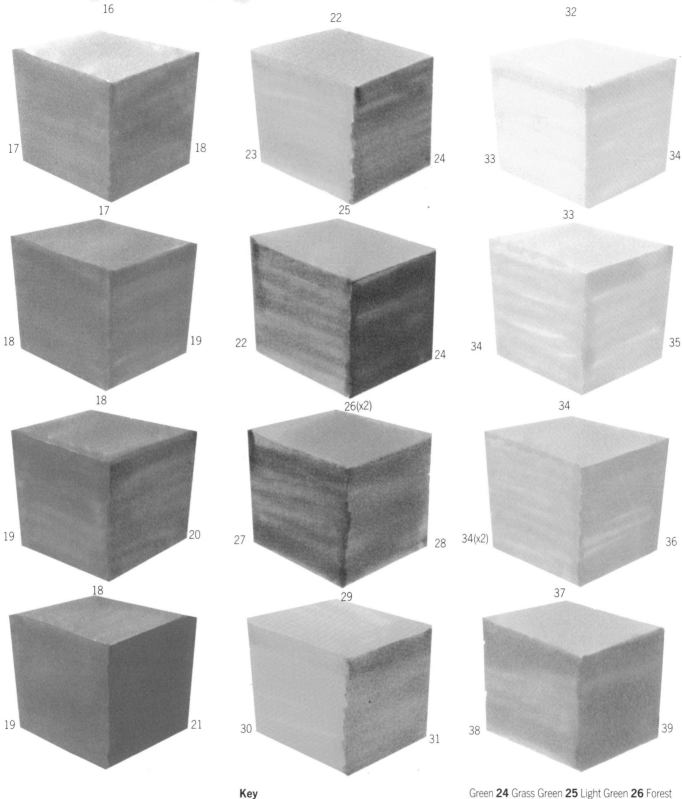

16

17   18
17

18   19
18

19   20
18

19   21

22

23   24
25

22   24
26(x2)

27   28
29

30   31

32

33   34
33

34   35
34

34(x2)   36
37

38   39

Key
1 Pale Rose 2 Geranium 3 Lipstick Orange 4
Vermilion 5 Red 6 Cadmium Red 7 Venetian Red 8
Lipstick Red 9 Carmine 10 Crimson 11 Deep
Magenta 12 Red Violet 13 Cadmium Orange 14
Chrome Orange 15 Sanguine 16 Pale Blue 17
Manganese Blue 18 Pthalo Blue 19 Mid Blue 20
Blue 21 Antwerp Blue 22 Pale Green 23 Marine

Green 24 Grass Green 25 Light Green 26 Forest
Green 27 Pinetree Green 28 Olean Green 29 Aqua
Blue 30 Scarab Green 31 Teal Blue 32 Pale Yellow
33 Process Yellow 34 Cadmium Yellow 35 Yellow
36 Yellow Orange 37 Barely Beige 38 Light Suntan
39 Dark Suntan.

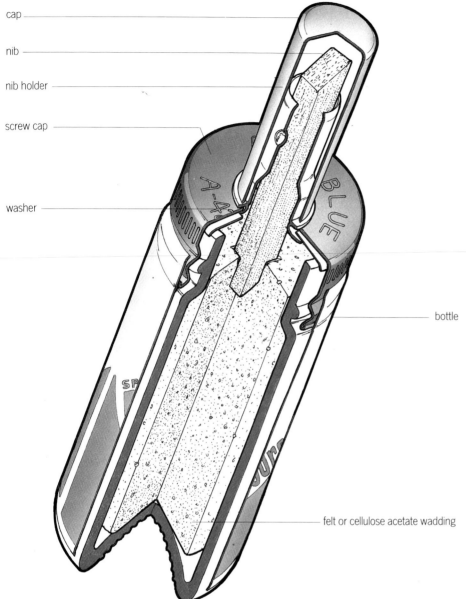

cap

nib

nib holder

screw cap

washer

bottle

felt or cellulose acetate wadding

find yourself using one type most of the time and reaching for alternatives in the few cases when a particular colour is only available in a different brand. The colour chart on pages 12–13 shows how a single brand of marker (in this case Magic Markers) can be used for three-dimensional modelling. Most experienced artists and designers will not need this chart, but for the beginner it should save a lot of experimenting in the graphics store. For the professional, you should restrict yourself to 'art' or 'studio' markers, so-called because they are available in a selection of more than 100 colours. Any brand that offers less than this is inadequate for most visualizing, and you will find significant gaps in its range. When choosing a brand, make sure that you try all the different types that are readily available from your nearest supplier – don't fall for a marker that is only available by mail order from a stockist the other side of the country, as they always run out at the most critical moment! See which ones feel comfortable to use and suit your own style of drawing and try to talk to experienced artists about why they use particular brands. Look also at the work they produce – assess the quality and finish and compare it with your own requirements. When testing markers, see how they perform in the following key areas.

Colour range

As already discussed, you need a comprehensive range of colours. This should include a range of warm and cool greys in at least five, and preferbly nine, shades. Make sure that you have a good range of pale shadow colours: pale blues, greys, and flesh tones, etc., as you will find that these are more in demand than any of the other colours. This is because they are used for delicate modelling on white paper where the bleed-out to white needs to be subtle.

This cut-away view shows all the parts that go to make up a Magic Marker. The manufacturing tolerances and quality control need to be very tight to prevent loss through evaporation and on-shelf deterioration. The felt wadding can be eased out with a scalpel and held in a bulldog clip for use as a giant marker.

Selecting a brand

There are so many different brands of marker to choose from that the beginner is often at a loss when it comes to knowing what to buy. Every experienced artist and designer has a favourite brand, and even the launch of a scintillating new range of markers will not tempt him or her to change. The main reason for this is that he or she has built up experience with the product and is familiar with the colours and the exact results. This predictability is vital for the busy marker artist and the prospect of changing to a new brand is very daunting. This section therefore includes a survey of marker characteristics against which a beginner can measure the performance of individual types of marker. Of course, it is not necessary to restrict yourself to a single brand, but in practice you will

A selection of other solvent-based markers. When starting out, try one from each brand and see how you get on with it: above all, talk to someone who is very experienced and get the pros and cons well sorted out before committing to a range. Note the excellent and unique extra-wide and wide Illustmarkers from Japan.

Left: a selection of the water-based markers available. Staedtler fine-liners are available in a good range of colours. The unusual Mars brushpens have some of the feel and quality of a traditional brush because line thickness can be easily adjusted by delicate changes of pressure and angle on the tip.

Markers are available for marking in many different types of media on various surfaces—from concrete to glass. Shown below are some of the more unusual types found in the graphic studio. In paint markers the medium is not held in a tampon—because it is opaque and free flowing, it requires a valve action in the tip and an agitation ball in the reservoir.

Consistency and continuity

If you buy a marker from your local graphics supplier and the same colour from a shop the other side of the country, or you compare a new marker with one that has been around for a couple of years – assuming it is well sealed (and many manufacturers do guarantee their products for shelf life) – you should expect identical colours from each. However, some manufacturers have better quality control than others, and because markers are batch-produced there is always a risk of inconsistency. Colour continuity refers to the colour remaining the same throughout the life of the marker. Some colours of certain brands have a tendency to separate in hard use or when they have been left around for a while.

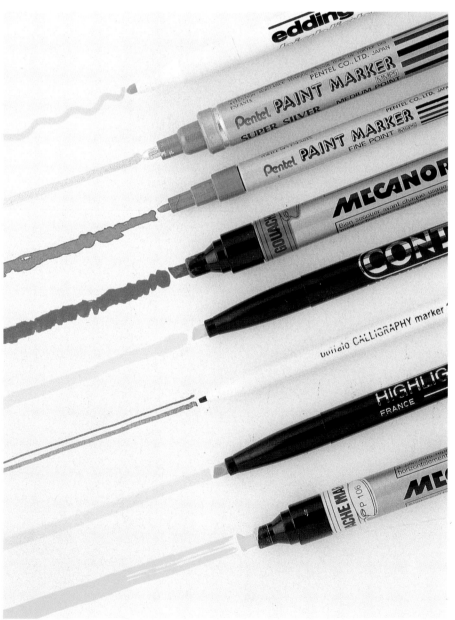

Nibs

The most commonly used nib shape is the chisel. This is because it offers the greatest flexibility by allowing three different line thicknesses when used on each of its faces. Many brands are also available in bullet, fine and extrafine nibs with colour consistency across all types. Some newer types have a different nib shape at each end which guarantees colour consistency as they both draw from the same reservoir.

Nibs are made in a variety of felts and synthetic fibres, with most early examples made from the former. Felt has its fibres randomly disposed in the material. As a result, it tends to produce a less controlled flow with more bleed and blodge, but this does depend on the density of fibres and how hard they are packed together. Synthetics can be configured like a felt nib to give similar results, or with the fibres running predominantly in the same direction which gives good control over the ink flow. The harder the nib the better the line definition, and the softer the nib the easier it is to produce fields of flat colour. A soft felt nib will bleed but will allow more subtle blending of colour as the ink pools, whereas a harder nib will bleed far less and be more difficult to blend. A hard nib will also feel unsatisfactory and can even scratch the paper.

So, ideally, you need a nib somewhere between the two extremes. To some extent your choice will depend on your style of work: if you favour tight, controlled drawings go for a harder nib, and if your work has large fields of blended colour, err on the soft side.

The AD Marker from the USA, below, is unique in having interchangeable nibs which can be changed quickly and easily for different effects. The nibs are available in Fine, Bullet, and Chisel shapes and are simply slotted into the nose; this is best done with a pair of tweezers to avoid hard-to-remove ink staining the fingers.

Above: every artist and designer has favourite tools, but be careful when choosing plastic rulers, sweeps, curves, and ellipse guides. Most solvents in markers attack many plastics (particularly acrylic), so excessive use with a marker will cause the edges of tools to deteriorate and become difficult to clean.

Ease of use

Ergonomically the marker should be easy to manipulate, so the more pen-like it is the better. However, the most important factor is colours that have a name so that they can be lodged in your colour memory more easily. When working, you know exactly what type of colour you want for a particular area; you dive into your memory and come up with a name – say, Venetian Red. Without this descriptive tag it is very hard to remember the differences between shades of colour. (The colour accuracy of barrel printing can't be guaranteed.) The name becomes even more important in a busy studio when a colleague calls for a particular colour. Short dumpy markers have two main advantges: they make colour selection easy and they don't roll off a crowded drawing board so readily.

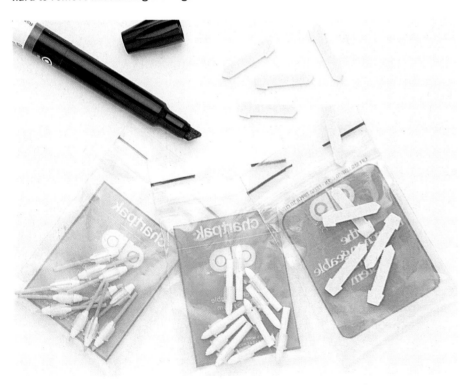

Some pieces of equipment, right, which are useful to have around. Good-quality marker paper is obviously essential, and a masking medium of some kind is necessary on large-scale drawings where you may be using the felt from inside the marker. Most important is solvent for cleaning tools and topping up tired or run-down markers.

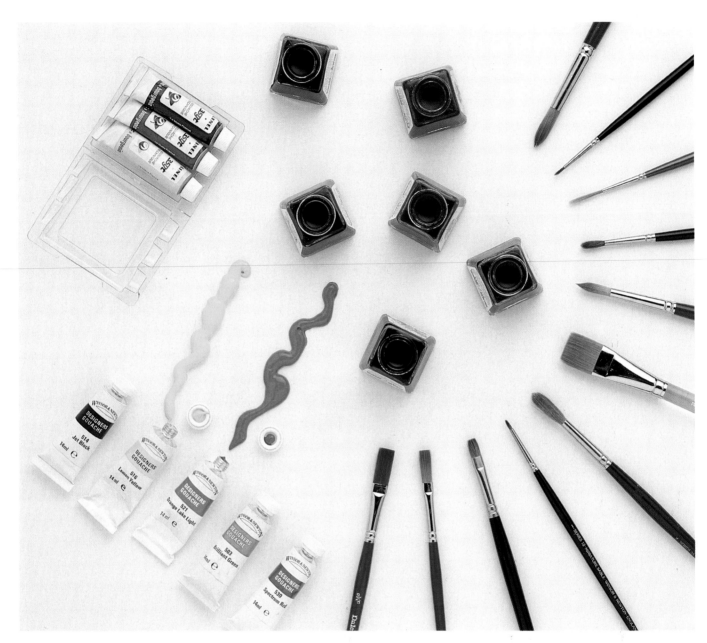

Markers on their own are rarely sufficient for producing visuals, and these two pages show some of the other materials which are often combined with markers.
Paint and brush: the traditional artist's medium without which no studio is complete. When choosing brushes, as with so much graphics equipment, it is sound advice to always buy the very best available. If you look after them, and never lend them to anyone, especially the colleague who leaves them overnight in the water jar, they will last a lifetime.

Systems
Many brands are associated with printing-ink systems, and offer a complete range of colour-matched products for every stage of the graphic design process. This can be very important for some type of graphic design, but is obviously less important to the vast majority of marker artists and visualizers.

Openability
It is extremely useful to be able to take a marker apart for two reasons. Firstly, to top it up with solvent – this allows you to keep paler versions of the original colour, and can save money by extending life (but be sure to keep topped-up markers separately, or well identified, from fresh

ones). Secondly, it allows the tampon to be removed, held in a bulldog clip, and used like a broad brush; this is absolutely essential for creating large fields of colour.

Starting out
The question asked most often by students is 'what colours should I buy to begin with?' The answer, inevitably, is that it depends on what you intend to draw. However, I usually recommend a starter pack consisting of three Cool Greys (2, 5, and 7), three Warm Greys (2, 5, and 7), a Black, a Pale Blue and some primaries. Thereafter, you should concentrate on colours that work well when blended close together – buy *groups* of markers rather than individual colours, and practise using them together.

Looking after markers

It is a good habit to always re-cap markers immediately after use and not leave them open, even for short periods: the solvents are extremely volatile and will evaporate very quickly if left exposed. Many artists keep semi-dry markers for special effects, while others can tolerate nothing but brand new full-flow ones. An apparently 'dead' marker may in fact only have a dried nib (if it has a glass bottle this can be established by checking the wetness of the tampon through the base). In such a case the marker can easily be revitalized by a drop of solvent on the nib to re-establish capilliary action. Never put in more solvent than was there originally, or the marker will bleed profusely. The amount you should add can be established by trial and error for your brand, but about 5 cc is average.

Paper

Of all the other materials you will need, the most important is paper. Again, personal preferences will dominate your choice, but some broad advice is useful for the beginner. Special marker pads are recommended as these are usually treated on the back to prevent bleed-through to underlying pages. The whiter the paper is, the more brilliant the colours will be. This is especially true of back-coated papers, as the colour is retained in the top sheet. On the down side, the whiter the paper, the less opacity it has for tracing through from sketches and underlays. If you favour a loose, sketchy finish with a lot of blending, choose a lightweight paper which will puddle more easily, but if you want a tight, bright drawing go for a slightly heavier, whiter, and back-coated paper.

Coloured pencils are useful for tidying up blurred edges and adding to the tonal values of the marker. Also shown here are Faber-Castell Polychromos Pastels, much favoured by automotive designers, which are used for expanding tonal range and for achieving an airbrush-like effect.

2 Techniques

Marker is an efficient, rewarding but limited medium – it does a certain job and does it well. To use it effectively you need a direct, bold approach and, as with any medium, the more familiar you are with it, the less you will have to think about the mechanics of what you are doing and the more freely you will be able to work. In this chapter we look at some of the techniques available to the marker artist.

Marker marks

The range of markers available to the artist and designer is constantly changing and expanding. Manufacturers make slight adjustments to existing products and launch new ones, so it is almost impossible to describe and discuss all the products on the market. There are four broad categories of pens with porous points: wedge-tipped studio markers; markers with broad bullet-shaped nibs; fineliners; and brushpens.

Here we have concentrated on the wedge-tipped studio marker which is the basic tool of most visualizers, and many designers and artists. The nib of the studio marker is made from felt or a synthetic equivalent. The beauty of this marker is its versatility, for the wedge-shaped nib gives you two or three different lines. A broad line, useful for laying down large areas of colour, is created by using the flat, chiselled end and a sideways motion. By turning the pen over and using the very tip you can make a thin, even line. A third line is created by using the chiselled base flat on the surface and

making a lengthways movement. You need to be familiar with the tool, and know exactly which way to lay the point on the paper, to be able to exploit the full range of marks – some of them require a bit of thought and practice. When you are working to a deadline it is useful to be able to get as many different marks as possible from a single pen – it saves time and limits your overheads by keeping to a minimum the range of materials you have to keep in stock. However, the bullet-shaped pens, fineliners or brushpens can be useful additions to your collection – which you use will depend on your technique and on the brief.

Markers with a broad bullet-shaped tip offer a narrower range of marks but are better for detailed work, and where the quality of line is important. However, it is much more difficult to lay down a large area of flat colour for you almost inevitably end up with a streaky effect. This is not necessarily a disadvantage: you may not need to lay flat colour; you may want a streaky effect; or you may prefer to lay flat colour with another type of marker, such as

the broad Illust markers by Holbein; or you may want to use an airbrush.

Some artists, however, use only brushpens or the finer markers or fineliners. Here, we show a brushpen, a particularly useful pen with a long flexible nib which bends like a brush and creates a sinuous line with thicks and thins. The fine point is excellent for detailed work.

What you require from a marker will depend on the purpose for which you use it, on your technique and on personal taste. Your choice will also depend on your experience – there is a tendency to stick with what you are used to, and if you work in a studio it makes economic sense to use the same materials as everyone else. However, markers do vary from make to make: some have a broad unyielding nib, others are more pliant; some have a huge range of colours, whilst others are more limited; some have a particularly good selection of greys or make colours that are particularly useful for certain purposes. Here we look at the marks that can be made with some typical products.

1 Magic Marker Slimgrip pen. This has a long, round, barrel and exactly the same chisel nib as the traditional Magic Marker. It is also available with a fine point.

2 Swan-Stabilo STABILayout marker. This has a water-based ink, and the wedge-shaped nib is more finely chiselled than the Magic Marker. The flat shaft is designed not to roll.

3 AD Marker by Chartpak. This is a water-based version with a wedge-shaped nib. As with other wedge nibs, it is possible to get an intermediate-width vertical stroke. The broad line is wider than the other markers shown here.

4 Magic Marker studio marker. This has a wedge-shaped, synthetic nib exactly like the Slimgrip marker shown in the first picture. It is chiselled, but the drawing tip is not as narrow as the STABILayout.

5 Pantone Marker by Letraset. This nib is chiselled, and the felt tip is narrower than the AD Marker's tip. The barrel is long and slim, and the rectangular cross-section prevents rolling.

6 AD Marker by Chartpak. This is the permanent version of the pen shown in picture 3. Both pens have interchangeable nibs. The barrel is long, slender, and round in section.

7 Interchangeable nibs by Chartpak. From left to right: fine; bullet; wedge; brush. This extends the range of marks, but changing the nibs is messy and you have to wait for the ink to soak through.

8 Marsgraphic 3000 water-based brushpen by Staedtler. This allows the artist to produce thicks and thins rather like a paintbrush.

Gutting a marker (right)

You will probably need to lay a large area of flat, untextured colour from time to time – for a background, for example. The speed at which you can lay colour is limited by the size of the nib. Some markers, such as the Japanese Holbein Illust marker, are available in very broad sizes so that a large area can be covered with a few strokes. If you cannot find one of these, take a Magic Marker, and open the bottle to remove the felt inside. The wet felt can then be used to paint a large area of smooth colour very quickly. To remove the felt use the technique described here, or hook it out with a scalpel. The process is fairly messy, and if you don't want to get your fingers stained the felt can be gripped in the jaws of a bulldog clip. The felt can be replaced in the bottle after use but bear in mind that if you have covered a large area you will have used quite a lot of ink, so the marker will be drier.

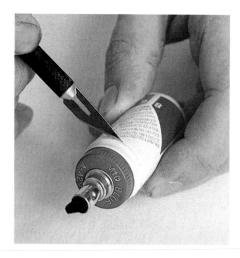

1   Grip the marker firmly and, using a knife, cut the seal just below the rim of the cap.

2   The cap can now be twisted off, revealing the felt within the bottle.

Using a gutted marker (below)

The gutted marker allows you to work very quickly with wet colour. This means that colour can be laid over a large area – an A2 sheet, for example. It also lets you create very subtle effects, especially if you use non-bleed paper and work into an area which has been dampened with lighter fuel or a solvent such as Flowmaster. Using the marker felt in this painterly way you can create texture, subtle tones and blended colours. The translucency of the medium resembles watercolour, but the colour dries very fast, allowing you to lay on the next layer of colour almost immediately, so that the image builds up quickly. We illustrate some of these effects later. In this sequence of pictures we show you some of the marks that can be achieved with a gutted marker.

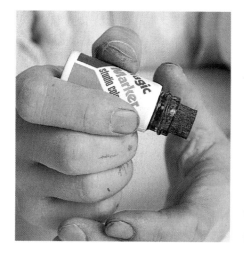

3   Hold the bottle in one hand and knock both wrists together to dislodge the felt.

4   The tip of the felt can now be gripped and removed quite easily.

5   The edge of the marker felt can be used to create a fine line.

6   The round end is used to lay a broad strip of solid colour.

7   A wide band of colour can be laid using the length of the marker felt.

Laying flat colour

Often, you will need to lay an area of flat colour with no variations of tone. This is quite simple once you know how but, like all marker rendering techniques, requires a knowledge of the tool you are using and a bold, direct approach. Markers are designed for speed and part of their attraction is their rapid drying time. However, this creates its own limitations. It is, for example, difficult to blend colours and achieve subtle gradations of tone. You must work quickly if you are to overcome these restrictions.

When laying flat colour it is important to work fast and keep the front edge of the colour wet, picking up the wet edge on the return stroke to avoid streaking. The edge of the colour must not be allowed to dry until the area is filled in. If you are dealing with a complicated shape you will need to plan the application of colour so that you do not work yourself into difficult situations which give you too many wet edges to maintain. You can avoid this by cutting a mask which will allow you to work freely, or by laying down the colour very broadly and cutting the shape from the flat colour.

The best results will be achieved by using a new marker, especially if you want to cover a big area. Markers get used up and become dry, causing streaking, which makes the ink look lighter. This variation of tone is quite important in some applications. In animation studios, for example, markers are sometimes used for colouring in backgrounds. But as there must be continuity of colour from frame to frame the artists keep on using new markers, so that for a single sequence they will use several of them – a very expensive process! So when you want to lay a large area of flat, even colour use a new marker which will give you wet, saturated colour. But save your old markers. Artists generally have markers of various ages in their collections – they all have their uses, as you will see.

2 The ADmarker has a slightly broader nib – work quickly and keep the edge wet.

The type of marker you use will dictate the way you lay flat colour. Magic Markers, for example, are quite good for laying flat areas as the fibres in the nib allow the ink to flow quickly and easily, but the AD Marker has a slightly broader nib so it covers a large area with fewer strokes. Illust markers by the Japanese company Holbein, are available in very broad widths which make them especially suitable for laying wide swathes of colour. However, it is not always possible to have a particular colour in a particular width to hand. In such circumstances, you will have to lay the colour with your usual wedge-tipped marker. Remember that Magic Markers can be gutted and the felt used in the way described on the previous page.

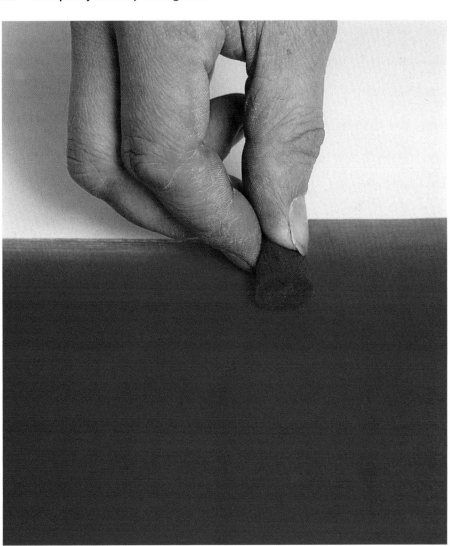

1 Using a Magic Marker work briskly from left to right, keeping the front edge wet.

3 A felt from the ink well of a Magic Marker allows you to fill an area quickly.

Building up tones

Marker is a transparent medium and in many ways resembles watercolour. In order to describe form you need to establish a range of tones, but with marker you cannot mix colours as you can with paint, so you have to develop a different method of working. Most manufacturers produce markers in quite extensive ranges of colours so you can select different tints of the same colour and work as you would with pastel, laying down patches of colour alongside each other. You will soon become familiar with the colour charts of your particular marker. Magic Marker, for example, produce a range of nine warm greys and nine cool greys and about 19 shades of green from Blue Green, through colours like Spanish Olive, to Grass Green. Pantone have a similar range of greens and slightly more greys.

Another way of building up tones and mixing new colours is by exploiting the transparency of the medium, which allows you to lay down a colour and

Here we see just two tones of a single colour. The artist laid down an area of flat colour using a Light Blue Magic Marker on Daler-Rowney layout paper. This was allowed to dry completely and the second layer of colour was then applied over the first. The transparency of the ink means that one layer enhances the colour of the overlying layer, creating a darker tone of the same blue.

modify it by overlaying it with another colour or the same colour. This extends the range of tones and colours which you can get from a small range of markers – some artists use a very limited palette indeed. Even artists with a fairly extensive palette tend to have a few favourites – colours which they are constantly replacing.

The number of layers of colour that you can lay down depends on the type of marker and also to a very great extent on the type of paper. Layout paper is fairly absorbent and so the inks do not build up on the surface, making it possible to put down several layers of colour. Bleed-proof marker papers, however, do not absorb the inks so the layers of colour tend to accumulate on the surface and eventually the paper becomes saturated, the colour starts to puddle and dries with a sticky finish. Most papers will take two or three applications of the same colour, after that very little change in tone will be discernible. It is important to allow each layer of colour to dry completely before the next is applied, otherwise the underlying colour will be disturbed and you will not achieve a flat, even application. If you do find that the surface is becoming tacky a fine dusting of talcum powder will reduce the stickiness – or a light rubbing with a putty rubber. On some papers yet another layer of colour can be applied on the reverse side – not on marker paper, however, which has a non-absorbent underside that will not take marker. This technique works very well on vellum, a semi-transparent tracing paper which is more absorbent than ordinary tracing paper and has a great deal more tooth and is therefore more suitable for markers. Both sides of the paper are alike, but the marker ink does not penetrate the paper, although the colour shows through, and another layer of colour can be applied on the reverse.

Bleed or bleed-proof paper

Most marker work is done on layout paper. It is light and fairly transparent which allows the artist to trace off from underlays. However, it does have a degree of opacity – it is more opaque than tracing paper, for example – and this gives the paper a whiteness which provides an excellent foil for marker inks, especially when it is mounted on a white surface. Layout paper is fairly absorbent and marker ink bleeds through the paper, usually staining several sheets beneath the one you are working on, and these then have to be discarded. You can minimize this by placing a sheet of non-absorbent material, such as tracing paper, beneath.

Marker used on ordinary layout paper tends to have a flat, rather matt appearance, which is ideal for certain applications. However, if you want to build up really brilliant, saturated colours you should use one of the special 'bleed-proof' or 'non-bleed' layout papers such as Letraset marker paper. These papers are coated on the underside to prevent bleed-through. This protects the underlying sheets but, more importantly, because the colour is

retained on the paper surface, marker used on this type of paper retains more of the vividness of ink and has more colour impact. Bleed-proof paper tends to dry more slowly than ordinary layout paper. This is because the ink is not absorbed and drying therefore occurs by evaporation alone rather than by a combination of absorption and evaporation. Also, the paper cannot take as many layers of colour and may sometimes begin to break up after more than four or five applications – it depends how wet the paper gets. The surface of some marker papers is easily damaged by masking tape so make sure that you use a low-tack tape or film.

Whether you opt for ordinary layout paper or for the bleed-proof type will depend on the finish you require – you might use layout paper for blocking in loose backgrounds, exploiting the bleed to achieve softly blended effects. The bleed-proof paper might then be used for more detailed work that requires crisp edges and accurately defined marks.

Special bleed-proof or non-bleed marker papers have two surfaces. The underside of each sheet is coated with a material which acts as a barrier to marker inks. If you have to tear off a sheet from your pad, to work on a Grant projector, for example, you should mark the top surface in some way. One young designer didn't do this and made an elaborate pencil drawing on the wrong side of the marker paper. When he started to apply the marker colour he found that it wouldn't take and realized his mistake – as a reversed image was not acceptable he had to trace it off again, involving himself in a lot of extra work.

Some manufacturers such as Frisk produce a double-sided marker paper which is bleed-proof, but which can, nevertheless, be used on either side. Most are single-sided, but check.

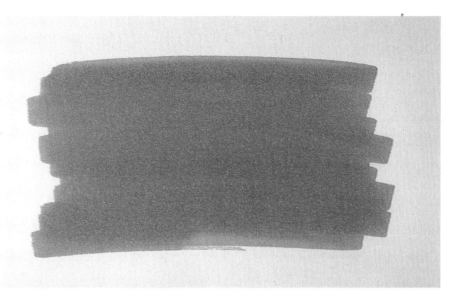

1   Left, the artist has laid a flat area of Magic Marker Pinetree Green on the right side of a Letraset marker pad. The coverage is good, giving an area of flat, intense colour.

2   In this case (right) the same colour was applied to the coated side of the marker paper. If you compare this with the previous picture you will see that the colour has broken up, giving uneven coverage and a textured finish.

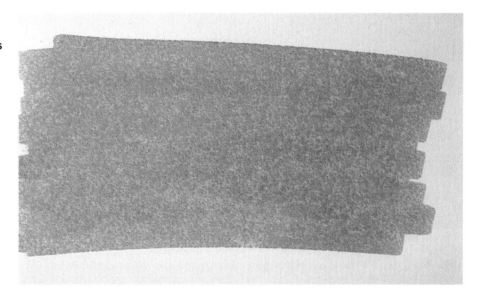

3   If ink is applied to the wrong side of the paper it is not permanently fixed, and can be removed by gentle rubbing (left). In general, this is not desirable — especially when several hours have been spent working up a visual!

Achieving a crisp edge

Markers are used for a great many purposes – we illustrate some of this versatility in the later chapters of this book. The common feature in most marker work is that the artist or designer is required to work quickly – this is inherent in the nature of the instrument, but time constraints are also imposed by clients. The marker is used to develop and progress ideas, to give them a concrete form, to 'visualize' them so that other people, often visually illiterate, can assess, approve or reject them. The marker artist is not usually required to produce a technically accurate drawing, his brief is to create an illusion, and as the visualizer's work is usually 'binned' afterwards it does not have to stand the detailed scrutiny an illustration or a technical drawing might be subjected to. The marker artist tends to look for shorthand ways of expressing the visual world and for shortcuts which will speed the production of the visual. These become part of his or her stock-in-trade. We will see many examples of these techniques and devices in the illustrations in the later chapters of this book.

Here, we look at a subject which involves a series of interlocking colour areas, with crisp, clean edges. There are three possible approaches to this problem. The first is to produce an outline drawing in pencil and to infill this with colour (see opposite). The way in which you work must be planned carefully if you are to maintain a wet edge and avoid working yourself into impossible corners. It may be possible, for example, to disguise marker edges against a highlight or some other feature.

It is difficult to lay absolutely flat colour, for the momentum with which the colour is applied is constrained by the outline. In order to achieve a really even application of colour it is necessary to develop a regular rhythm, for as the stroke decelerates more colour is applied. Really skilled and experienced artists will be able to cope with this, but it might be worth considering masking the colour areas (see below). By masking the area the colour can be applied freely, with the deceleration occurring over the mask.

Yet another possibility is to lay areas of colour, cut out the shapes and assemble the images. An image produced in this way has a specially crisp quality.

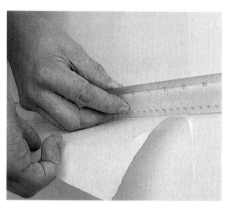

1 Low-tack masking film is laid onto layout paper. The artist pushes the film with a ruler, while pulling the backing.

3 The film is then peeled, very carefully, from the area to be markered. Lift the film in one corner and pull gently, making sure that the paper is not torn.

5 When this first application of colour is dry, the artist turns the paper through 45 degrees and repeats the process.

2 The artist cuts the mask, using a new blade and very little pressure. With an old blade too much pressure will be applied and the cut will reach the paper beneath.

4 Here, the artist lays Cadmium Red, working briskly down the sheet and keeping the edge wet.

6 When this is dry the mask is peeled off, revealing a square of red which is flat and even with neat, crisp edges.

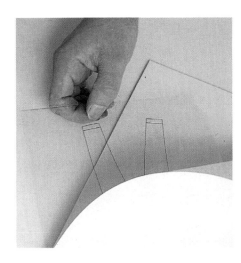

1   The original is placed under a sheet of Letraset marker paper and the artist traces it in pencil.

2   He removes the original and goes over the pencil drawing with a Sandfords Expresso fibre-point pen. He uses this for the outside lines to give them weight.

3   Here, the artist uses a Nikko finepoint pen for the inside lines. He starts the line from both ends, bringing them together in the middle – this avoids blobbing.

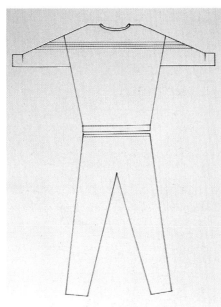

4   Different pens have been used to vary the line widths. The Nikko finepoint is one of many pens of this type. It has a plastic tip and is available in six line widths. The metal collar is ideal for using against a straight edge.

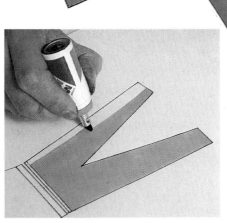

5   The shape to be coloured is uncomplicated and the artist works quickly, from top to bottom. This gives him a long, but simple wet front.

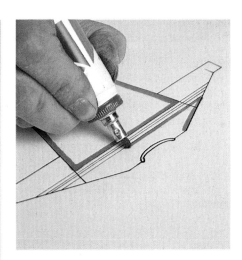

6   The artist runs the marker around the edge and then works from side to side, keeping a wet front. If you work towards the centre the wet edge will be too long.

7.   The final image is simple and effective – but compare this with the version on the next page.

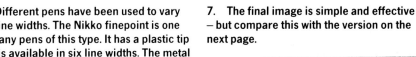

Using separate elements

In the previous project the image was developed as a single unit, by infilling a line drawing. But it is difficult to maintain the momentum of the stroke within so confined an area, and some of the colour is slightly streaky. Here, the same project is tackled in a different way. The artist starts by laying three areas of flat colour. He works in one direction first, turns the paper and applies another layer of marker to achieve dense, even colour. He then cuts the separate elements from the coloured papers and assembles the image. This procedure has two advantages: it is quick and produces a crisp, clean image.

2   The shapes are traced off in pencil and then cut out using a sharp scalpel.

3   The separate elements are fixed to a sheet of layout paper.

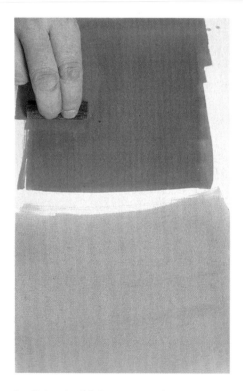

1   Using the felt from a gutted marker three areas of colour are laid down. The second layer is laid across the first to create an even, untextured finish.

4   The final image (right) is clean and effective. It was put together very quickly – compare it with the image on the previous page which was put together much more slowly.

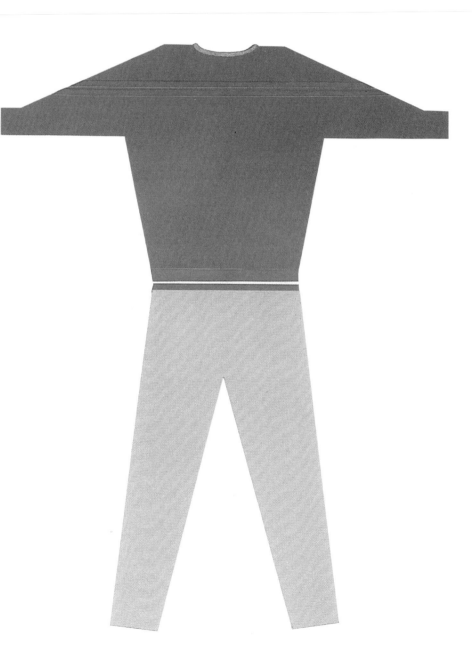

Reviving a marker

Markers are expensive and so there is an economic incentive to extend their useful life. In constant use they are viable for a very short time, but they don't run out suddenly, they gradually become drier. Run-down markers do have their uses and most artists have a stock of them which they use to create streaky highlights, reflections or textures. The life of markers with screw tops can be further extended by adding marker solvent, Flowmaster or lighter fuel to the felt wick inside. Ideally, you should use the marker solvent produced by the manufacturer of your brand of markers, so that the flow characterstics of the marker remain the same. Although lighter fuel is an easily available alternative it will have a different flow rate, and will bleed more, or less, depending on the marker brand. Make sure that you do not overfill the marker (4–6cc maximum for a Magic Marker) or the marker will flood. To avoid confusion, mark the revived markers so that they are easily distinguished from new ones. The colour of the revived marker will be lighter than the original, thus a C3 Cool Grey becomes a C2. Here, we compare the colours produced by a new, a dry and a revived marker.

1   A few drops of lighter fuel are applied to the felt inside a Magic Marker.

2   The dense, even tone of a new and wet C3 Cool Grey Magic Marker.

3   Below, the streaky, uneven coverage of a dry C3 marker.

4   Above, when lighter fuel is added to the dry marker the colour produced is no longer streaky, but it is lighter in tone. So a revived C3 looks more like a C2.

Laying a fade

In many ways marker is a limited medium. Each marker contains only a single colour which dries quickly with a clearly defined edge. It is difficult, therefore, to blend colours or to achieve softly graduated tones. Artists overcome these limitations by combining marker with other media, or by devising techniques which extend the possibilities of the medium. Here, we demonstrate a technique which is useful for skies, backgrounds or other large areas where a gradual lightening of tone is required.

1 The materials used for this exercise are layout paper, tracing paper, lighter fuel or art cleaning fluid, cotton wool wipes, a scalpel and a selection of Magic Markers. Lighter fuel is a petroleum-based product and should only be used in a well-ventilated room away from any naked flames.

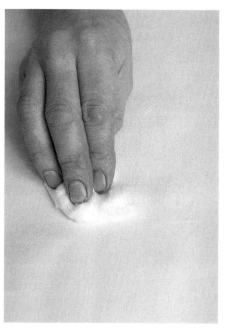

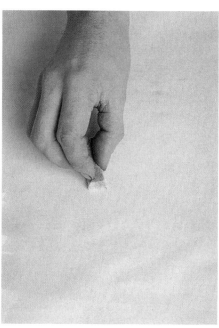

2 The artist works on a Daler layout pad which has a very absorbent surface. He places a sheet of tracing paper underneath to act as a barrier and retain the lighter fuel and marker ink in the top sheet. Here, he sprinkles lighter fuel over the centre of the top sheet.

3 The fluid is spread evenly over the paper with cotton wool. Speed is necessary as both petrol and marker ink evaporate rapidly and the success of the technique depends on the paper being wet.

4 Here, the artist puts down a wash of Brick White, the lightest colour in the Magic Marker range. This knocks back the paper colour.

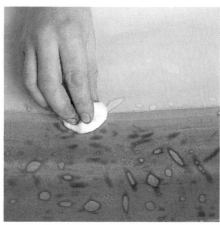

7   Left, the dark blue is drawn down into the pale blue. If the paper has dried, the artist will sprinkle more petrol onto it. The inks must be kept wet if a subtle blending of colours is to be achieved.

8   Below, using this technique the artist has achieved three bands of colour – dark blue, pale blue and beige – which blend gradually into one another, with no harsh edges.

5   Above, more fluid is sprinkled over the paper, then the artist lays a wash of Pale Blue onto the wet paper, again spreading it with cotton wool. The colour is taken down into the Brick White. At this stage the paper is flooded with petrol and marker, so he is careful not to tear it.

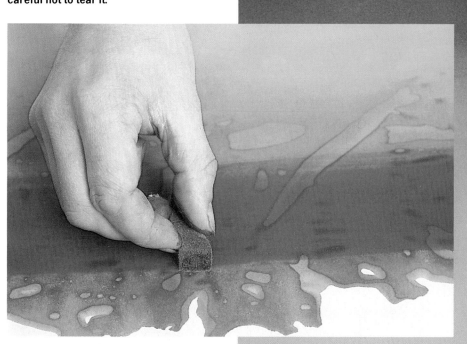

6   Above, the artist adds the darkest colour, Peacock Blue, dotting in the colour with a felt from a marker.

Rendering wood

Marker artists are often required to render wood or wood-type surfaces. The accuracy of the rendering and the amount of detailing required will depend on the application, and will vary from brief to brief. In an ideal situation the artist would find a wood sample in order to get the colour, texture and graining right, but photographic reference gleaned from magazines is also useful. Often what is required is merely a suggestion of the correct colour and texture, and most experienced artists have a formula for depicting wood which can be modified slightly for each application. By changing the colour and the graining pattern they can represent the light, densely grained surface of oak, the creamy, knotted surface of old pine, or the rich russets of mahogany.

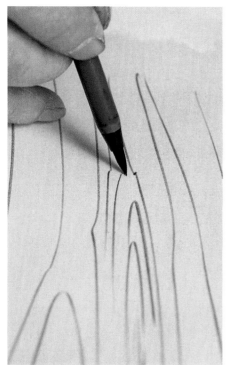

2   Above, he works over the yellow with the felt from a dry Light Mahogany marker. Dried markers give that streaky effect which captures the texture of wood. Here, he adds more graining in Dark Brick Red marker.

3   Left, the tones are beginning to build up, giving the subject density and depth. The underlying yellow shows through, giving it that gleaming quality typical of old polished wood.

1   Mixing media (above) is often the best way of tackling the subject quickly—here, the artit has combined brushpen, dried marker and pencil. He starts by laying down Buttercup Yellow, working quickly to keep the colour flat and even. Then he uses a black brushpen to draw in the grain of the wood.

4   Right, the artist applies streaky colour to build up the density and variety of tones. Again, he uses the felt from a gutted marker. The marker is old and fairly dry, so this streaky effect is automatically achieved.

5   Left, white pencil is skimmed across the surface to create highlights within the veining of the wood. The white lines are knocked back by rubbing them with a finger.

6   The technique is both fast and convincing. By using the same approach and modifying the colours and texture, it is possible to suggest a variety of woods.

Rendering metal

Visualizers are often asked to produce gleaming metal surfaces, particularly chrome. To create a reflective surface they identify a light source and look for contrasts. The white of the paper may be left to stand for the highlights, but gouache or another opaque medium can be used to create sparkle.

1   The artist sketches in the main outlines in soft pencil, then lays in dark tones with black fineliner. Black marker and a dark grey brushpen are used for the reflections in the headlamps and the chrome.

2   Above, the mid-tones are blocked in with a selection of markers, making sure the highlights are maintained.

3   Below, the dark tones beneath the vehicle are added. A bleedproof white paint is used to touch in highlights.

Rendering plastic

Plastic is another material popular with today's designers and manufacturers. Visualizers and designers are often required to provide a client with a visual of a plastic product so that they can assess designs and colours. They will also be asked to provide visuals for advertisements and television commercials.

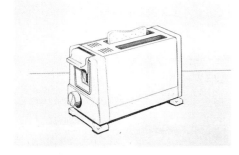

1   Above, the artist uses fineliner for crisp fine lines, and marker for the darkest tones.

2   Right, the broad areas of local colour are blocked in.

3   Above, with marker it is possible to build up layers of transparent colour, creating flat colour which, nevertheless, has depth. Here, Pale Rose has been overlaid with Warm Red to give a warm, matt red for the plastic ends of the toaster. On the Venetian blinds Cool Grey (C5) has been laid over Light Blue, darkening the tone beneath each slat. Finally, the corners and edges which catch the light are given a white highlight with gouache, applied with a fine sable brush.

4   Right, we see the final image, with a mask dropped over it, for presentation to the client. The visual gives him an excellent idea of how the proposed colour schemes and decorative detailing will appear.

Rendering glass

Glass has always presented the artist with a challenge – even the Old Masters demonstrated their virtuosity by including glass objects in still-life studies. The secret is to combine areas of high contrast with subtly graded blues and greys – here, the artist has used powdered pastel applied with cotton wool to create a vignetted effect.

3 The bottle is laid in with Forest Green, and the wine with Cadmium Red and Venetian Red, which is taken over the bottle green.

4 Highlights are touched in with white gouache, and white pastel is smeared on with cotton wool to create gleaming highlights in the glasses.

1 The artist starts by creating a graded background. He begins by laying down Pale Blue, using a gutted marker. Over that he lays Cool Greys (C2, C4 and C7).

2 He then draws in the outlines of the glasses and bottle using a brushpen, which gives a crisp but variable line width. The dark tones are touched in with Cool Grey (C4) and the very tip of the marker. Shock Pink is used to add warmth to the base of the glasses. Pale Yellow is laid loosely over the bottle and the liquid in the glass. This will add warmth and substance to the final colour.

5 Right, we see the final picture masked for presentation to the client.

Rendering marble

The technique for creating a marble effect is really very simple. The base colours are laid down, and then lighter fuel or some other solvent is sprinkled over the surface, dissolving the colour, causing it to puddle. It dries to create the blotchy, uneven colour typical of marble—which is difficult to render in any other way.

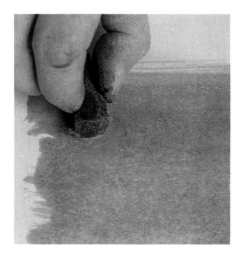

1   Using a gutted marker, the artist lays down a broad area of Steel. He works quickly to cover the entire area, though in this case an entirely flat finish is not necessary, for inconsistencies will become part of the marble pattern.

2   The attractions of marble are its colour, the way different colours combine in a variety of patterns, and the veining which runs through it. Here, a second colour is introduced—the artist lays streaks of Teal over the base colour.

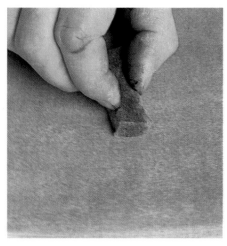

3   Another layer of Steel is applied.

4   Below, lighter fuel is sprinkled over.

5   Below, the lighter fuel has dried, leaving the surface marked with patches of lighter colour. Here, the artist uses a white pencil to trace in veins.

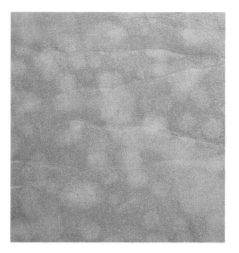

6   The white veining is knocked back by rubbing it gently with the fingertips. The marble effect, above, can be created with any combination of colours.

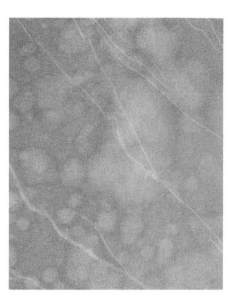

7   Above, we show another example of marbling—this time the artist used Mauve shadow as a base, and then applied streaks of Light Blue.

Rendering flesh and hair

Here, the artist shows us how marker, which is a fairly crude medium, can be used to render delicate skin tones and the fine texture of hair. Brushpen is used for the outlines, and for working up the texture of the hair. It is a useful medium which combines well with marker, supplying a degree of detail which is impossible to achieve with the wedged nib. It also has a flowing, responsive line which is ideal for this type of application. To achieve softer, blended effects the marker is first applied to cotton wool and then dabbed onto the paper, creating softly modulated colour with no hard edges.

1   This is the first rough work-out.

2   Using the first drawing as a trace, the artist lays in the linework using a selection of Staedler Marsgraphic brushpens.

3   The artist blocks in the basic local colours, ignoring tonal variation at this stage, but remembering to leave the white of the paper to stand for the highlights down the side of the face. The colours used here are Brick Beige for the skin, with Pink and Vermilion for the fabric, bangles and flowers.

4   Below, brushpens are used to develop the lights and darks in the hair. Light Suntan is used for the flesh mid-tones.

5   Opposite, Venetian Red is added to the folds of the fabric, and Light Suntan to the arms and the hair. The high points of the cheeks and forehead are warmed with Pink.

3 Projects

Marker is a fast, energetic medium, requiring nimbleness of mind as well as manual dexterity if you are to get the most from it. Its speed and flexibility are the factors that recommend it to the designer and to the artist preparing presentation material. Marker is superb for fast rendering of coloured visuals and is used by many artists because at the moment it is the best tool for the job. But in the commercial world commitment to a product depends entirely on results, and as soon as a better medium appears markers will be abandoned. So far, to the great relief of the manufacturers, nothing better has come to the fore although computer-aided design may supersede them one day—but that time is still a good while off.

The great advantages of markers are their simplicity, the speed with which they dry and the extensive choice of colours available in any one range. They are compatible with other media, can be used on a variety of surfaces, and are extremely convenient—you will not need brushes, palettes or pots of diluent, and will not have to waste time cleaning up.

The ink is contained in a reservoir in the barrel so that they are clean and easy-to-use, like a pen, and they require no fixing. However, markers do have limitations: for example, you cannot mix colours, and the range of marks is limited by the shape of the nib, though manufacturers have been fairly ingenious in designing the drawing points, and artists have been even more ingenious in exploiting them. Many people also find the solvents in which the dyes are dissolved extremely unpleasant—even if you are not particularly bothered by the smell you should make sure that your workplace is well ventilated.

Markers are expensive compared to many other media and are considered a medium for the 'commercial' rather than the 'fine' artist. But in the commercial world where time is money, and the client is prepared to pay for high quality presentation material, marker has no competitors—at the moment. Presentations are extremely important in a competitive world, where we are exposed to increasingly slick and high quality visual material—on television, in advertising, magazines and so on. The marker offers the designer and the client the opportunity to see a convincing colour rendering of the product, whether a bicycle or a television commercial, before committing themselves to further costly development. Markers are excellent for their purpose and artists and designers, being an inventive breed, have devised many ways of overcoming their limitations. The way that practising artists exploit the medium and overcome its limitations is what this book, and this chapter in particular, is really about.

The term 'marker rendering' suggests that there is only one approach to the medium, but each artist develops his own particular way of handling marker, his tricks-of-the-trade. Certain techniques become popular in a particular studio, for artists and designers working alongside each other inevitably exchange ideas—this is rarely a conscious process, but seems to happen by a sort of intellectual osmosis. However, artists from different studios or from different industries rarely have the opportunity to exchange ideas. This is because, unlike most other manifestations of the visual arts, presentation work has a short life: once it has served its purpose and the deal has been clinched, the commercial made or the magazine put to bed, the visuals are 'binned'. Work is sometimes shown in trade magazines, but generally there are very few places where visualizers, and marker artists in particular, can see the work of others in their field, so the exchange of ideas tends to be within a fairly small circle. When researching the material to illustrate this book we found that much good work had been

irretrievably lost, we also found that certain techniques and styles were peculiar to a particular field. Sometimes these characteristics were obviously related to the function of the drawing—automotive designers, for example, are particularly concerned with rendering reflective surfaces, and have developed a range of techniques using airbrush, powdered pastel and talcum powder. But often it seemed that the style and techniques were traditional in that area—we hope that this book will both inspire and offer the opportunity for cross-fertilization.

In this chapter we look at several projects in detail and see how a single image can be created from separate elements. This compilation method exploits the best talents of the studio and allows a presentation to be put together very quickly. We also look at projects in which pastel, gouache, pencil and airbrush are combined with marker to increase the range of the medium. In the final project we see a complex subject evolve from preliminary sketches to a highly finished image—the degree of polish may surprise those of you who think of marker as a medium for rapid and very sketchy notations.

Cityscape

In this project the artist wanted to show a generalized cityscape with towering buildings against a vivid sunset. He simplified his task by treating the foreground and background as two entirely separate elements, only bringing them together at the very end. This allowed him to work more broadly, freely and quickly than if he had developed the image as a single unit. An image of this type might be set by an agency art director – and art directors are always in a hurry. The visualizer is merely his 'wrist', putting his ideas down on paper, so that he can assess their effectiveness and show them to others – the client for example. Often several ideas will have been mooted, and the visuals allow the agency and client to compare and judge them. What is required is a fast, convincing two-dimensional representation of a concept. The marker artist assesses the brief, identifies the problems, decides how he will tackle it, looks for reference if he needs it and sets about creating the image. He does not have time to experiment, but uses techniques which he knows will work.

2   The felt is removed from a Sanguine marker and this is used to dab in the forms of the clouds. The gutted marker is a less precise tool than the wedge-tipped drawing point, and is ideal for laying in less defined shapes and for building up subtle colour effects.

3   Here, a Dark Brick Red marker is used to lay in darker tones within the cloud formation. The artist dots in the colour using the very tip of the nib. He allows the marker to rest on the paper for a few seconds so that colour flows from the felt onto the paper, creating imprecise patches of colour rather than a series of dots.

1   The background was laid onto a Daler layout pad – this paper bleeds, but is excellent for the blended effects the artist wanted to achieve. He used the technique described on pages 32–3 in the section on laying a fade. The colours used were Magic Marker Pale Yellow, Pale Rose, Sepia, Brick Red and Peacock Blue.

4   Process white is applied with an airbrush to create the disc of the sun, its halo and the underlighting of the clouds (right).

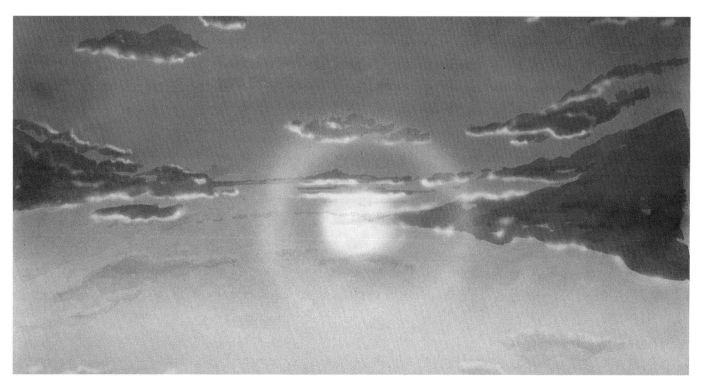

5   The detail above shows just how simple the techniques are on close inspection. However, it is not the details which are important but the overall effect. Through his knowledge of the medium the artist has achieved maximum effect for minimum effort.

7   The drawing is then used as a trace, and is slipped under a sheet of marker paper. Below, the artist lays in the important structural lines with a Marsgraphic brushpen, which gives him thicks and thins.

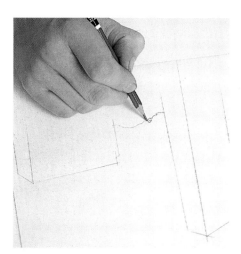

6   Above, the artist lays in the foreground drawing on a separate sheet of paper, with an HB pencil.

8 Using a dry, and therefore streaky, Pale Blue marker, the artist lays in the sides of the buildings. He works quickly, and having decided his method of attack he does not hesitate. Marker is not for the faint-hearted!

9 A felt from a new, wet marker is used to lay in solid blocks of Pale Blue for the front planes of the buildings. The artist works quickly and is not concerned about overrunning the edges of the drawing, for the image will be cut from the paper at a later stage and this will tidy up the edges.

10 The foreground is blocked in with Light Green. Again, a stripped marker is used. Texture is then added to this area by scribbling on Forest Green.

11 Left, a wash of Pale Yellow laid onto the side facades of the skyscrapers suggests the setting sun reflected in the glass.

12 Above, the artist then lays Warm Grey (W4) over the front facades, applying the colour very briskly with the long side of a marker felt. Teal Blue is used to cool the shaded side of the buildings.

15 Left, the foreground is dropped onto the background and the artist then assesses the image as a whole. He decides to add impact to the foreground, and increase the sense of space and recession, by working into the bushes. He uses Pinetree Green to stipple the texture of foliage.

13 The glazing bars are drawn in with Dr Martin's non-bleed white, which covers any medium. Several other manufacturers produce a similar product. The colour is applied with a fine sable brush and a plastic ruler is used as a straight-edge.

14 Below, the image is fixed to a sheet of layout paper—to prevent show-through when it is attached to the background. The artist then cuts out the foreground using a scalpel with a new blade. He uses the knife to define and tidy the edges.

16 The final image (right) is an effective evocation of a cityscape with skyscrapers, theatrically lit by the setting sun. The artist has created the image in about an hour. By treating foreground and background separately he has been able to work with great freedom and speed, for he has not been concerned with the outline, knowing that the image will be dropped out at a later stage. The only problem with working in this way is that the separate elements may lack coherence, but if this should be the case it can be set to rights later.

Marble figure

In this demonstration the artist takes us through the evolution of a fantasy image: a marble figure set against a dramatic sky. This is the sort of image that visualizers are often requested to create by art directors – for magazine or newspaper advertisements, for example. The artist was asked to assume a very tight deadline and use as many shortcuts as possible. The background was developed quite separately from the foreground. He started by laying a fade using the technique described in the previous chapter. The clouds were dabbed in with a gutted marker and their forms were then firmed up using Stabilotone pencils. These are fat pencils, produced by Swan-Stabilo, which combine many of the qualities of coloured pencil with those of pastel and watercolour. The leads are 10mm thick, and soft, allowing the artist to lay in a lot of colour quickly. The colours are watersoluble and may be blended with a wet brush. The figure was traced from a 1960s magazine photograph and then marbled using the technique described previously. The two elements were then cut out and assembled by pasting them to a sheet of paper. The entire visual was completed in less than an hour.

1   Working from suitable photographic reference, the artist dabs in the broad forms of the clouds using a dryish felt from a Pale Blue marker. Used conventionally, marker is limited by the dimensions of the drawing point – by taking the inside out, the artist has created soft, rather formless colour areas.

2   Using the soft pastel pencils the tones within the clouds are hatched in. He uses four colours: white, grey, pale blue and (above) dark blue.

3   One of the advantages of these pencils is that they are watersoluble – here, a moist brush is used to soften and blend some of the hatched marks.

4   In this detail you can see the way in which the flat, translucent marker colour contrasts with the opacity of the pencil. The lightly applied pencil pigment sits on top, capturing the fluffiness of the clouds.

5 The figure was traced from a 1960s magazine, using a Marsgraphic brushpen to give a fluid line. The trace was then put under a projector and taken up 30%.

6 The image was placed under a sheet of non-bleed paper, as a guide. The paper was soaked with solvent and Light Green marker was layed onto the wet surface.

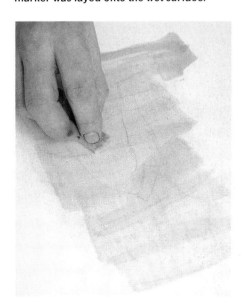

7 Streaks of Pink were then laid over the green, again using the felt from a gutted marker. Lemon yellow was applied in the same way.

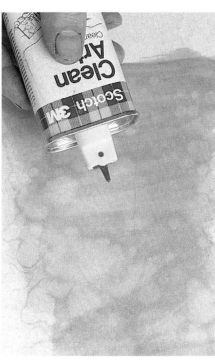

8 Here, the marker is spattered with lighter fuel or solvent. This dissolves the ink, causing it to puddle in a random way which suggests the texture of marble.

9 A brushpen is used to trace the outline. We have now the basic form and texture of a figure in marble – it has taken the artist about 15 minutes to reach this stage.

10 Using the tip of a Light Green marker the artist dabs in the darker tones, softening the edges with solvent-soaked cotton wool.

11 The foreground is laid in with Forest Green, using the felt from a gutted marker. He works broadly, using the felt to lay flat colour and draw out the forms of grasses.

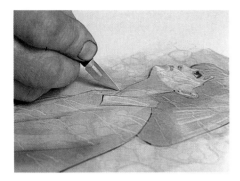

12   Using a sharp scalpel the artist cuts around the outline of the figure. In this detail you can see a white veining in the marble, laid in with a white pencil.

13   The artist uses a dark green brushpen to darken the cut edge of the paper.

14   The figure is dropped onto the background and fixed with an aerosol adhesive. Here highlights are painted into the grasses with Dr Martin's non-bleed white.

15   The final image is a striking and evocative visualization of the initial concept. By working broadly with gutted markers and adding details with soft pastel pencils, the sky was laid in with great speed. The figure was treated in a similar way: using reference, laying in broad areas of colour with marker, using a trick-of-the-trade to create the marble effect, and adding detail and tone with the tip of a marker. The two elements were only brought together at the very end. But by working on them separately the artist was able to work with a freedom, and at a speed, which would not be possible had he attempted to treat the subject as a single element.

Landscape

In this project the marker is used as a painting medium to create a subtly blended landscape, using mainly gutted markers, with brushpen, pastel pencil and gouache for detail and texture. The final image has a painterly quality, typical of watercolour rather than the graphic character we have come to expect of marker. To achieve this effect the artist worked on layout paper, laying a sheet of tracing paper under his working sheet to protect the rest of the pad. He is looking for a soft, blended effect, rather than crisp edges and lots of detail, so the absorbent nature of the layout paper is appropriate in this instance. The technique involves the use of a lot of solvent or lighter fuel so ensure that your work area is well-ventilated, and extinguish all naked flames.

Marker dries more quickly than watercolour, so the artist needs to be alert and have a deft touch to lay down and blend colours before they dry. He exploits the transparent quality of the colour, overlaying one with another to achieve a third, and so extends the range of his palette.

1 A brief sketch is made with a sepia brushpen. Lighter fuel is sprinkled on and **Brick White** is applied to the wet paper and then spread with a cotton wool pad.

4 A warm grey **(W2)** is used for the underside of the clouds. A wash of **Mauve Shadow** and **Brick White** is laid over the bottom of the picture.

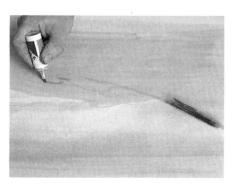

7 The shadows on the side of the mountain are laid in with **Lavender** and **Mauve Shadow**, using the marker to lay patches of colour and squiggly lines.

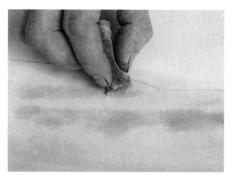

2 While the paper is still wet the artist works into it with **Mauve Shadow**, creating flat colour at the top and bands of colour lower down.

5 Here, the artist dampens a cotton wool pad with solvent and then dabs the felt of a **Chrome Orange** marker onto the wet pad, so that it becomes saturated with colour.

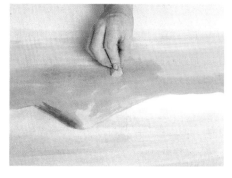

8 **Pink** is used to knock back the **Chrome Orange**—again the marker is stripped and the felt is used to achieve broad coverage of freely applied colour.

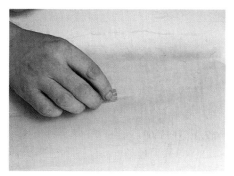

3 **Cadmium Yellow** is dropped in and blended with a cotton wool pad. Then, using the side of the marker, he dots in the brightly lit edges of the clouds.

6 The pad of cotton wool is then used to lay a wash of colour over the landscape: the area is quickly covered with a streaky layer of orange.

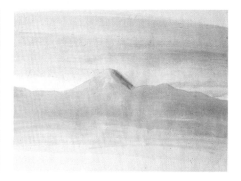

9 Here, we can see the progress of the image—the combination of flat colour, blended tones and streaky linear effects.

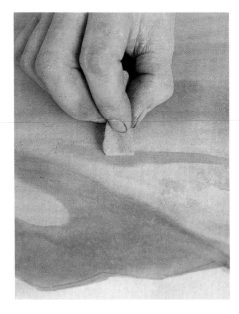

12   The visual is not quite finished but already the landscape is convincingly rendered, the overlapping colours implying recession towards the horizon.

15   The warm brown band in the foreground, and the simply rendered strip of trees and shrubs, give the painting a sense of scale and depth—compare this with picture 12.

10   The paper is again wet with solvent and a Pale Blue felt is used to lay in patches of shadow on the hillside. The colour is then brought down into the foreground.

13   To enhance this sense of recession the artist now works into the foreground, adding detail to bring it up to the picture plane. Here, he adds Marine Green touches.

16   A wad of cotton wool is dampened with solvent and Lilac marker is dabbed into it. With this, the artist lays colour across the middle distance.

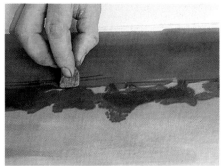

11   A Cool Grey (C3) is used to tickle in small patches of shadow and to sharpen the edges of the shadows. By emphasizing the contrast subject brightness is heightened.

14   A warm orange—Dark Suntan—is laid across the foreground, over the greens and blues and lilacs, which add depth to what would otherwise be flat colour.

17   Right, the artist is satisfied with the broad outlines of the image, and starts to lay in the final touches. He uses an orange brushpen to lay in linear details.

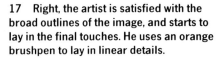

18   A brown brushpen is used to define the outline of the mountain, and details of rocky outcrops.

19   White and lemon gouache are used to lay in the capping of snow on the summit of the mountain. The creamy opacity of the paint contrasts with the flat marker work.

20   The tops of the clouds are picked out with a thick pastel pencil—again the change of texture adds interest to the picture surface.

21   Pale blue pastel pencil is scribbled lightly over the marker, so as to modify the underlying colour, rather than obliterate it.

22   Right, the final image illustrates the subtlety of tone and colour that can be achieved with marker.

Red car

This project was to be a visual for a press
advertisement for *Car Magazine*, where the final
artwork included a studio shot of the car. The
project was fairly typical in that the artist had to
work from a variety of material. He had a
photograph of the estate version of the car, but with
old styling on the front. To supplement this he had a
photograph of the new model – but taken from a
different angle. He had to create the rear of the
saloon version of the car from memory. Using the
photograph as a basis, he built up a preliminary
drawing by tracing the outline on a Grant enlarger.
He then incorporated all the details from the other
sources. When the drawing was resolved, the
perspective correct and so on, he used the first
sketch as a trace and transferred the image onto a
new sheet of Letraset marker paper. Remember
that the image is a visual, intended to test the
effectiveness of a proposed newspaper ad – it is not
a technical drawing and it would be inappropriate to
spend time working up a technically accurate,
measured drawing.

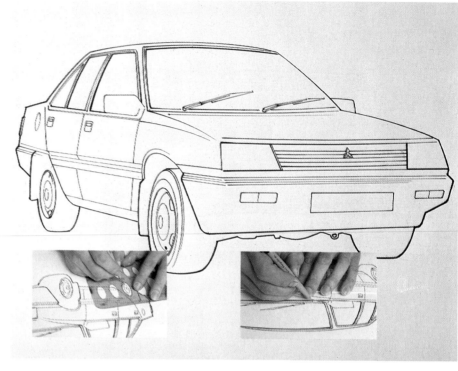

**2   The artist dampens a wad of cotton
wool with lighter fuel. A marker solvent
could also be used.**

**3   Pink marker is applied to the damp
cotton wool – in this way the artist creates a
10% tint of colour.**

**1   Working quickly from the reference
available, the artist put together a drawing
of the car. He did a rough in pencil so that
he could check the perspective, viewpoint,
detailing and so forth, and make changes
as necessary. A technically accurate
drawing was not required, but the car had
to look convincing – any gross inaccuracies**

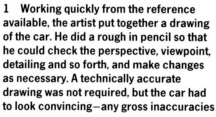

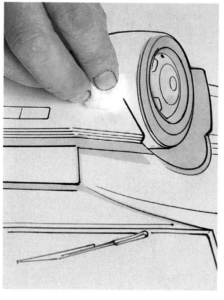

**4   With this 10% tint the artist blocks in the
darker areas of the vehicle, applying the
colour quickly and freely.**

would jar. Using his rough as a trace the
artist made a drawing of the car, using a
finepoint marker. The subject calls for crisp
detail so he used drawing aids such as
ellipses and straight-edges.

**5   The pink underpainting will give warmth
to the subsequent shadows. By building up
colour in layers the artist gives the colour
depth and body.**

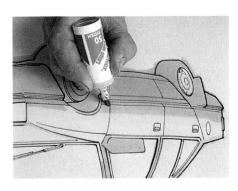

6   Lemon Yellow is now laid in as an underpainting for the Geranium which will be used for the side panels and the roof. The yellow will add substance to the red.

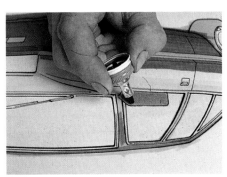

9   Here, the artist uses the lid and drawing point of the marker to colour up small details such as the wing mirrors.

11   Here, Cool Grey (C6) is used to define the details of the wheels. It is important to capture the changes of tone if the forms are to be rendered with any conviction.

7   Geranium is laid over the yellow. The artist works quickly for he wants flat unmodulated colour without tide marks.

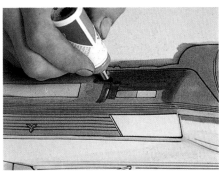

10   The detailing on the front of the car is added with Cool Grey (C6). In this detail you can see the way in which the pink modifies and warms the cool greys.

12   Here, the artist blends the colour by rubbing it with his finger. This blended edge contrasts with the crisp edge on the inside of the wheel.

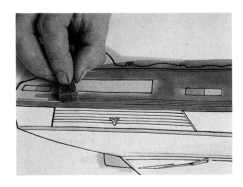

8   The felt of a C4 Cool Grey is extracted from the bottle and with this the artist lays in the shadow areas of the vehicle.

13   In a subject such as this (right) the broad forms and the details are equally important: both contribute to the individuality of the vehicle.

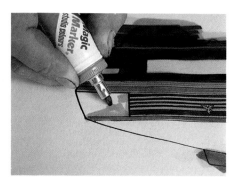

14   To capture the glittery effect of the textured glass in the headlamps the artist dabs in Warm Grey (W4), Mauve Shadow, Cool Grey (C4) and a little Yellow.

17   At this stage the artist has established the main elements of the bodywork, but the most reflective surfaces have yet to be tackled.

18   The artist decided to airbrush the highly reflective top surfaces, and lays Frisk masking film to protect the rest of the image.

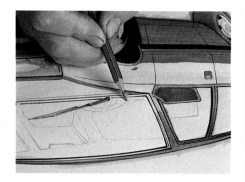

15   The broad outlines of the car interior are sketched in with a soft pencil (2B). Use minimal pressure, otherwise the pencil will leave an impression.

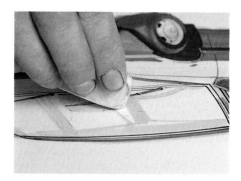

16   The interior is blocked in with a Pink marker and the pencil lines are then erased. Cool Grey (C4) is applied over the Pink.

19   The paintwork is airbrushed with bright red gouache. To achieve a gently curved reflection the artist uses a sweep as an edge to spray against.

21   Below, the inside of an appropriate ellipse is used as a template for the crisp highlight just above the wheel.

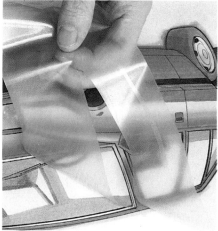

20   Right, when the paint is dry the masking film is removed – it lifts from paper that has had marker applied to it more easily than from non-markered paper.

25   The car is now complete and the artist proceeds to airbrush in a graded background, with dark tones under the body of the vehicle.

22   The subtle tonal changes of the glossy paintwork have been rendered with airbrush—later we shall see powdered pastel used to achieve the same effect.

23   The image is cut from its background, working carefully with a sharp scalpel. The image can then be applied to a separately prepared background.

26   Text, display heading and image are assembled and mounted on the airbrushed background.

24   Crisp white highlights—on joint lines and tyre treads—are added with gouache and a fine sable brush.

27   The final visual gives the client an accurate impression of what the actual advertisement will look like.

Wagon train

We asked the artist, David Lee, to take us through the creation of a highly finished visual which included people and lots of action—the sort of thing he might be asked to produce for a typical client. It was a loose brief, but no worse than many he gets. He started by roughing out some ideas for us to choose from. For this exploratory stage he uses a thick felt pen—a Pentel sign pen. He works quickly with brisk fluid lines on layout paper, trying out compositional arrangements, looking at the way the images fill the space, the way they relate to each other and the shapes they make on the sheet. He establishes the basic proportions, and thinks about the way the subject is lit and the consequent distribution of lights and darks over the picture surface. Many of his images rely for their impact on the way he uses light to create atmosphere. However, the visualizer can cheat in a way that an illustrator cannot. His work is required to make an impact, to get over a message quickly and test out ideas—if the project is taken further the illustrator or photographer will have to deal with the restrictions of the real lighting situation.

1   As the artist feels his way around the sketch, thinking with the pen, the images begin to emerge. Notice the interplay of angles—the spear, the horse and rider, the soldier with the gun—all creating a sense of energy which is balanced by the strict horizontal of the horizon.

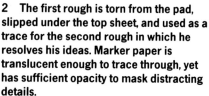

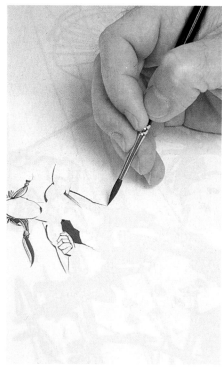

2   The first rough is torn from the pad, slipped under the top sheet, and used as a trace for the second rough in which he resolves his ideas. Marker paper is translucent enough to trace through, yet has sufficient opacity to mask distracting details.

3   The second rough is used as a guide for the final visual. The artist uses gouache for the underdrawing. In this example, a mixture of Winsor and Newton Flame Red and Ivory Black, applied with a series 7, number 2, Kolinsky sable.

4   The fine sable brush allows the artist to create thick and thin lines, which have a more fluid quality than line drawn with a marker. He uses the best quality sable and replaces them every few weeks, by which time they have lost the perfect point which he finds so valuable.

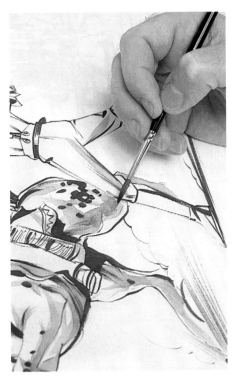

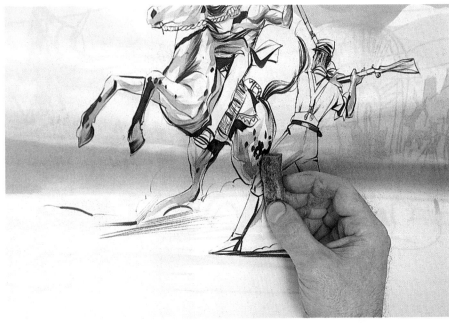

5   The artist uses the same number 2 sable and a wash of cerulean blue gouache for the shadows on the horse, and a mixture of orange and yellow for the torso of the rider—the wet wash creating its own texture. He does not feel that marker is capable of rendering the subtlety of skin tones which he requires.

6   The artist lays in the background in Mauve Shadow and Buttercup Yellow. He achieves a vignette effect by pouring a little solvent onto one end of the felt—this creates a lighter tone at one end, and a darker at the other. Above, he lays a band of Lipstick Natural with a gutted marker.

8   Below, the artist lays in the sky with Pale Blue and Phthalo Blue, using Mauve Shadow and a Cool Grey (C3) for the clouds. He has darkened the foreground with a layer of Africano—this would provide a suitable background for lettering. The wagons and other elements on the back-ground are laid in with Warm Grey (W4).

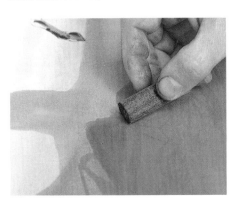

7   Above, the artist blocks in the foreground in Pale Sepia which has been diluted with solvent. He then applies a layer of Sanguine.

9   Here, the artist uses a Dark Suntan marker to block in the shadowy figure of the horse and rider in the background. He uses the marker to find the shape, working quickly, concerned to create a convincing silhouette which will have impact and reality without distracting from the main focus of interest. An illustrator would have to take this image further, resolving this figure perhaps. By using a pale colour and little internal detail the artist does two things—he suggests that the figure is behind the main group, and he starts to develop the illusion of dust rising from the trampled ground.

10   A group of figures on the other side of the central group are evolved in the same way, using Dark Suntan. He then brings these into focus by adding details with Warm Grey (W9) and Cool Grey (C9), thus creating the illusion that they are nearer to the viewer. In this way he very simply introduces a sense of space into the visual. He also touches in a few details to the wagons in the distance.
    Here, the artist uses a Flesh-coloured marker to fill in the torso of the Indian, leaving whites and light areas for highlights.

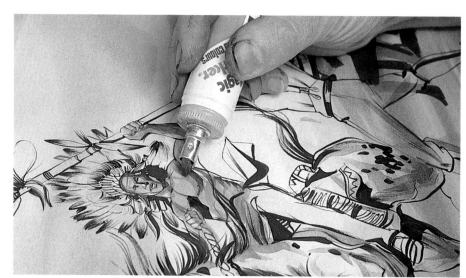

11   The soldier's trousers are laid in with Pale Blue, with Mid Blue for the darker tones. The jacket is a much darker—here the artist used Antwerp Blue. The artist is working from memory—he does not use reference because all he requires is an approximation of a soldier's uniform of the period. At this stage his client will be concerned with the overall effect rather than the details, but if a magazine advertisement, for example, were based on this visual, a great deal of professional time and effort would be spent getting these details right.

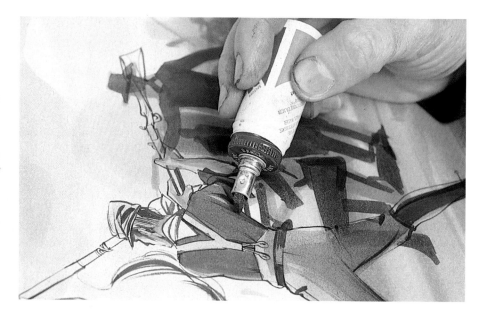

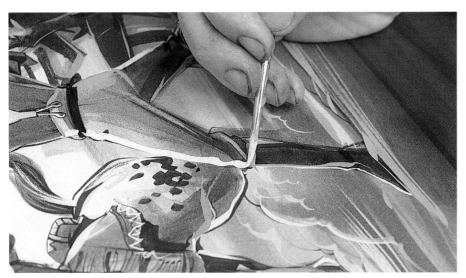

12   At this point the artist adds fine highlights on the horse, using a number 2 sable and white gouache. Here, he adds the trim to the soldier's uniform—this time he uses a mixture of lemon yellow and white. Marker is a transparent medium so you must work from light to dark—laying down your lightest tones first and gradually building up to the darkest tones. Light colours can modify a dark colour, but only slightly. So, if you want a light area you must either be careful to keep it light, or you apply a lighter tone later with an opaque medium such as gouache, pastel or pencil.

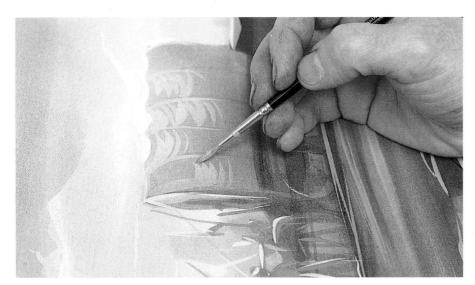

13   The figures and wagons in the distance are developed with touches of dilute gouache. The artist wants to sharpen up the forms without giving them undue significance. He views the image through half-closed eyes so that he can focus on the lights and darks, and lays in patches of colour, concentrating on broad planes rather than details.

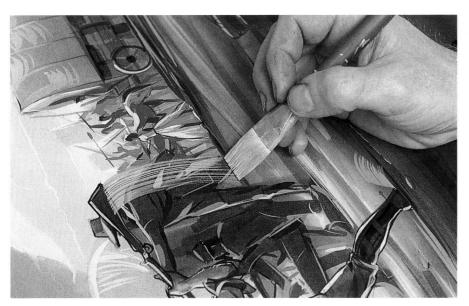

14   Here, the artist uses a dry-brush technique to create a strobing effect which suggests the upward swing of the rifle butt. He mixes white gouache with a little red ochre, loads an half-inch brush with paint and then removes some of the colour by dabbing it on tissue. This causes the bristles to separate and he then applies the colour with a single sweeping gesture. Practise several times before risking a nearly complete visual!

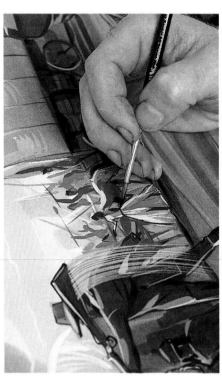

15   Here, the artist again uses a dry brush technique, but this time he is introducing highlights and texture into the rocky terrain in the middle distance. The effect of the drybrush technique is to create a less dense block of colour, so that the paint modifies rather than obliterates the previous layers.

16   The visual is nearly complete and the artist stands back and studies it carefully through half-closed eyes. He decides to develop the darker tones and add linear detail—here, he works into the distant figure group with a fine sable brush and black paint.

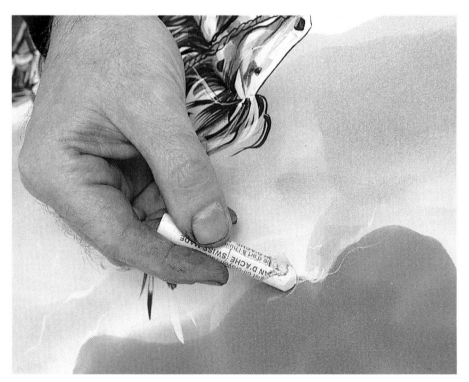

17   Left, Caran D'Ache pastel is used to soften the tops of the clouds, the opaque pigment adding textural interest to this area.

18   The final picture is highly finished and realistic. While working on the piece the artist relied on his magpie memory—the only reference used was the Indian's headdress. Marker allowed him to work quickly, laying down layers of colour and building up the tones. He used a fine sable brush and gouache at two stages: to draw the horse, rider and soldier group which form the focal point of the painting, and later, for details, contours and other linear elements which draw the image together. Throughout, he has been aware of the spatial elements and the lighting, and has concentrated on the central group, avoiding distracting details.

4   Advertising

Advertising is a high-octane industry – aggressive, competitive and very expensive. It employs the best people, works them hard and pays them well – but though the rewards are great the standards are high and schedules are gruelling. This is definitely not an area for the insecure or the work-shy!

The role of the marker artist in the wonderful world of advertising is an interesting one. Generally they work on a freelance basis, either directly to an advertising agency, but more often for a studio which offers them workspace in return for a first call on their services. The arrangements obviously vary from studio to studio, but generally artists will have their own clients in addition to the work that the studio puts their way.

Studios vary, some offer only visuals, others offer finished artwork, others specialize in an area such as animatics, and some organizations handle a whole chain of processes from conception right through to the production of a finished video. In fact each studio seems to have evolved its own particular way of operating, so it is difficult to generalize. It is also a fairly fluid field, with artists being enticed from one studio to another, and whole groups of people upping sticks and either joining other organizations or setting up on their own.

The artists themselves are a fairly unique breed in the field of art and design. They are a small and exclusive club, highly paid, with no special training and no particular career structure. They tend to know each other and can certainly recognize the work of their peers. Their most outstanding characteristic is their incredible ability. They are to a man and woman brilliant draughtsmen, able to create a stylish image with a marvellous economy of line. Only the very best survive for not only must they be able to draw accurately, they must also have a memory for detail and be able, and prepared, to work to exacting schedules. And these deadlines are really tight – often a job comes in and is out the door only hours later. An entire studio will work right through the night and over weekends to meet a deadline.

The best marker artists have a distinctive style – or possibly several – but they must also be able to collaborate on projects. If an 80-frame storyboard has to be put together overnight, the studio manager will delegate the work to as many as six artists. One will lay in the backgrounds, another will develop and draw up the characters, whilst another may lay in the colour. Finally, all the elements will be assembled and mounted together. In this arrangement there is no room for the cult of personality. The artist need not look for wide recognition or the kudos associated with being exhibited in galleries or reviewed and courted by the media. This is the ultimate in 'bin art' for no matter what creative, 'blood, sweat and tears' was involved, the work will end up in the dustbin eventually – and sometimes immediately. Despite their undoubted talent no-one outside the business

knows the name of a single marker artist or could recognize their handiwork.

But what exactly do they do, these self-effacing wielders of the marker? They visualize other people's ideas – visualizer is the generic term which accurately describes their trade or craft. Sometimes they work to fairly loose briefs, but often the briefs are quite specific and leave little room for creative input in the way of original ideas – the visualizer's genius lies in expressing the art director's ideas as literally as possible. In the business they are referred to as the art director's 'wrist' – he has the ideas, they put pen, or marker, to paper!

To an outsider it might seem profligate to expend so much time, creativity and money on artwork which may be presented to a client and immediately rejected. But the money involved in mounting a big advertising campaign, or putting together a television commercial, is so great that the agency, client and production companies involved must know that the idea is the right one: that it is going to work, pleases the client and convinces the target audience. The visualizer is in the communication business, allowing the creative people in an agency, for example, to express their ideas in such a way that the client, no matter how visually illiterate, will understand the concept. If the idea meets with approval the visuals can also be handed over to the production people – a photographer or film crew, for example, may be asked to work from a visual. In this chapter we look at some of the range of materials produced by visualizers: from roughs, through concept boards and storyboards to elaborate animatics.

Where do visualizers come from? Well, they certainly don't emerge fully fledged from the art schools – in fact very few colleges offer any training in marker rendering, probably because the very best artists are earning pots of money as visualizers and have no incentive to pass on their knowledge to generations to come. The artists come from a myriad of backgrounds – most of them have some sort of art school training, though by no means all. We've come across art school drop-outs, office messengers and ex-teachers who are now earning £60,000 to £100,000 as visualizers. The fledgling visualizer must above all be able to draw, and the dearth of drawing skills amongst college leavers is a constant complaint of studio managers – it takes at least a year to turn the most gifted student into a useful vizualizer. They learn on the job, working alongside experienced artists. There they pick up the tricks of the trade, those short cuts and professional touches which will allow them to produce a rapid but accomplished

rendering to a deadline. With constant practice, probably on the least interesting or rewarding projects, they will improve their drawing skills, their powers of observation, memory for broad forms and detail and their hand and eye co-ordination. And finally they will learn the possibilities of their chosen medium, and find ways of coping with its limitations.

We have talked to the artists and studios about each of the projects illustrated in the following pages: about the brief, the materials used and about their techniques. Marker is actually a crude and rather limited medium, but its outstanding advantage in this time-conscious industry is the speed with which a finished image can be rendered. Whilst artists are extremely inventive in the way they apply the medium, and resourceful in overcoming its limitations, the truth is that there are only a few basic techniques, tricks and shortcuts. In the final analysis the success of a visual depends on the interpretive and drawing skills of the artist.

Agency: MBA
Designer: Lindley Smith
Artist: Buz

This visual was produced for the cover of a catalogue for Pronuptia, a company which specializes in wedding dresses. The artist and designer had to work to a tight brief, because the client had a very clear idea of the feel he wanted carried from the cover right through the catalogue. This is the visualizer's interpretation of that concept, and was followed almost exactly by the photographer when the project went into production – even down to details such as the type of flowers in the model's hair and the freesia in her hand.

The artist started by preparing a pencil rough, which was then traced onto marker paper. The visual was rendered in Magic Marker, with white gouache for the highlights in the hair and the white flowers, and black fineliner for details such as the girl's eyes.

Roughs

The sort of material the studio receives from the client depends on the art director, the nature of the job, the time available, and how well the two organizations know each other. Sometimes the briefs are very skimpy indeed – perhaps a piece of A4 paper covered with what appears to be pencil doodles. For a TV commercial they might be given a script with the dialogue in one column and the scene description on the other. At worst all the studio gets is a verbal brief.

The first stage is to produce a series of roughs, often providing the client with several ideas to choose from. Roughs are produced for all types of work, including concept boards, storyboards, animatics, presentation visuals and cartoons. If the client is visually literate – an art director who is used to reading and interpreting visual material, for example – the roughs may be loosely drawn in black line. If the client is less used to dealing with visual material they will be shown a more finished rough, otherwise all sorts of misinterpretations and confusions can arise. No particular medium is used at this stage but marker has the advantage of allowing the visualizer to work up several ideas very quickly. Roughs can be in pencil, biro, felt pen – any medium which allows the artist to express his ideas, and allows the client to see and interpret them, will do. Sometimes the client will specify exactly what kind of roughs they want,

requesting colour and specifying the way in which they want them presented. This is often the case where an agency is dealing with a new client and wants to keep them involved throughout the development of the project. Sometimes roughs are used for market research and if this is the case the client will ask for more detail and a higher degree of finish. The emphasis placed on roughs may seem strange, but the rough is an important working tool. It is a way of working out ideas, and allows lots of people to have an input before too much time, effort or money is invested in a particular concept. A visualizer's time is expensive, and it is obviously cost-effective to have as many problems as possible resolved at these early stages.

Sometimes there will be several meetings and rough stages before the artist starts work on the final visual. On other occasions, when the team involved have worked together before, it may not be necessary to produce roughs at all, and the artist will go straight to the final visual. Again, time and knowledge of the client are important – but there may be several sheets of layout paper in the bin before even the first rough stage is reached.

Artist: Harry Bloom
Client: Spillers

These delightful doggy roughs (right) were for an animated film used in a television commercial promoting a canine product. The artist was provided with a script, and produced a series of roughs to show how the key frames would work. Though loosely rendered, the storyboard contains plenty of information about each episode. It shows how the pictures could be framed, how close-ups and long shots could be used, and the artist has also indicated the types of dog that might be included. Once he was satisfied with these Pentel roughs, the artist used them as an underlay for the colour visuals.

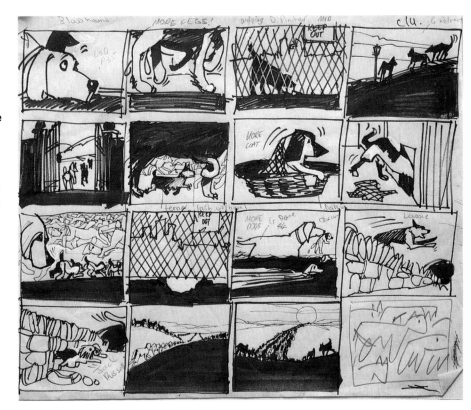

Artist: Harry Bloom
Client: Commadore Electronics

These roughs (right) were part of a project designed to teach children how to use video. The complete package included a book and a video, with the teddy bears being introduced to attract and hold the children's attention. The roughs were eventually worked up to full colour artwork rendered in marker, and in that form were reproduced in the book. This is rather unusual as marker is not generally used for finished artwork, although we do show examples in the chapter on illustration.

Artist: Harry Bloom

This vigorous work-out (left) for a King Kong storyboard was rendered with a Pentel sign pen – a fibre-tipped pen with an acrylic tip. This type of pen is designed as a writing instrument rather than a fine or graphic art medium, but it is a useful drawing and sketching tool with a pleasing quality of line, ideal for working up swift ideas. This type of black and white rough allows the artist to compose the picture. He organizes the elements within the frame, decides on the viewpoint, how much background will be included and so forth. Because it is a rough he can work freely, unhampered by the worry of making a mistake.

Storyboards

A storyboard, as the name implies, is a set of sequential frames which illustrate a story. The idea is to show a series of still images which depict the main features of a proposed project such as a video, a television advertisement, a film or an animatic. In the advertising field storyboards are usually related to animatics or television commercials.

There are several different kinds of storyboards, each with a particular use. Concept boards, which are usually produced at a very early stage, show how key episodes from a proposed project, a television advertisement, for example, might be handled. They may be fairly freely rendered, though at the client's request they may be more detailed. Their function is to establish characters, settings and the style of presentation before too much time has been invested in the project. This allows the clients to input their ideas, enabling the artist to then proceed with the work confident that his approach has been approved. If the project involves a particularly large storyboard the concept board may show two or three key frames. Not only does this give the client the opportunity to make adjustments, it also allows the artist to show alternatives if he finds that what the client has asked for doesn't work.

Shot and script storyboards are usually intended for presentation to the agency art director, or the art director at the production company. Again, the recipient is visually literate, understands what he is getting and generally requires a much less finished product than a client's marketing director, for example. These storyboards are working tools. They show the frames with the script in one-stroke lettering underneath each frame. Basically, one-stroke is a very neat form of handwriting used under each frame to show the dialogue which relates to it. It is used when there is not enough time to have the text typeset. Also, in many cases, the hand-drawn characters harmonize with the loose quality of a freely rendered marker drawing, in a way that crisp, typeset characters would not.

MVO: A STORYBOARD IS A ROUGH INDICATION OF HOW A COMMERCIAL WILL LOOK.

A SEPARATE FRAME IS DRAWN FOR EACH PART OF THE ACTION.

WHERE APPROPRIATE, THE SCRIPT IS WRITTEN BELOW EACH FRAME...

...ALONG WITH ANY SOUND EFFECTS.

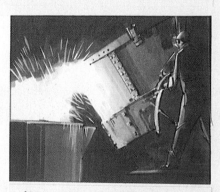

SFX: HEAVY INDUSTRY.

MVO: THE STORYBOARD IS THEN PRESENTED FOR RESEARCH.

Artist: Mark Bloom

Here, the artist encapsulates the main functions of a storyboard. His technique could be described as 'slick'. This is a much used term for which there seems to be no single definition, but we will return to this knotty problem later. The main elements are drawn in with a fine outline – here, he has used fineliner. The colour is then laid in briskly in fairly flat, rather simplified colour areas. In the first frame, for example, there is no tone at all, but in the third a little tonal variation is introduced to help establish the forms of the face. The message is clearly and simply put over, each stage of the action is accurately and realistically described, but the amount of detail is kept to the minimum required to convey the information. The technique has many of the qualities of a cartoon – outline and flat colour – but it is not humorous, and is quite straight-forward and unstylized. The heavy industry frame is dramatic, but the artist has achieved the effect with the minimum of detail. Notice the way the white of the paper has been left to stand for the brightest part of the image. Slashes of white paint laid over the marker describe the sparks from the furnace. Underneath each picture the script and sound effects are set out, allowing the client to relate sounds and words to a particular image. The letterforms used are clear and easy to read. This type of lettering is known as one-stroke, and often an artist specializing in this technique will be called in when a large job is involved. Each frame was drawn on layout paper, mounted on another sheet and then each frame was pasted separately onto a board. The one-stroke lettering was prepared separately and pasted under the relevant frames.

Another type of storyboard is much more highly finished, basically executed in marker but with a great deal of other media to work up details such as texture, tones etc. This type is usually intended for presentation to a client.

Working from the scamp and script provided by the client, the artist will draw up rough outlines for each frame, usually in pencil. This is the stage at which decisions are made and problems resolved. The artist will have to decide on the viewpoint for each frame if this has not already been decided by the art director. The perspective can then be sorted out. The appearance and clothing of the principal characters will have to be established at the

beginning, so that there is continuity throughout the storyboard. The pencil rough is worked on until the artist and studio are quite happy with it. In fact the people involved are such skilled draughtsmen, and are so professional, that the elements seem to come together remarkably quickly.

The pencil rough will then be traced off onto layout paper with a fineliner, or sometimes with a paintbrush or a brushpen. Once the outline is done it will be filled in with Magic Marker – the broad areas of colour and the lights and darks will be laid down. The level of finish depends entirely on the client – for in-house agency use it will be much looser than that required for presentation to an outside client. When a

big job comes into the studio and time is short, one artist may do all the pencil roughs – this establishes the style. Then to speed up the process several artists may trace off the frames, making sure that the consistency is maintained. Then, as each is completed, it will be passed to other artists to lay in the colour and add the final details. Sometimes different artists are used for different elements – some specialize in rendering pack shots for example, and that part of the visual will be left for them to fill in. Some artists are used primarily for their figure work, others for food. Usually these special areas require a great deal of fine detail, and are often rendered with a range of media, as well as marker.

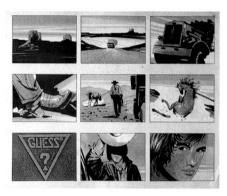

Agency: Gregory Lunn Challenge
Studio: Helicopter
Artist: Trevor Goring
Client: Guess

These are 5in by 7in frames from a series of storyboards which comprised 45 frames in all. The job was a jeans commercial for cinemas in the U.S.A. The product is an expensive, up-market, designer jean and the commercials reflect that image – the magazine advertisements use stylish black and white graphics. The artist was asked to supply a shot and script-type storyboard. A high degree of finish was not required as the storyboard would be used by the art director for the shoot – it would help him decide just how much film would be required, but would leave him plenty of scope for creative input during shooting. The artist laid in the outlines with fineliner for the thinner lines, and black marker for the thickest lines and darkest touches of tone. The colour was laid in with a limited range of Magic Markers – Buttercup Yellow, Pale Rose and Pale Blue. For their impact the images rely on the energetic and accurate line work, the high degree of contrast and the limited range of colours used.

Animatics

What is an animatic? It is actually a very simple animation. In an animation each stage of a movement is drawn up as a complete frame, whereas an animatic uses only one background and some moving parts. There are two stages in the creation of an animatic – firstly, the preparation of the artwork, and secondly the filming of it – each contributing to the degree of complexity of the final film. An animatic is really an animated storyboard. Indeed, a very simple animatic can be created by filming a storyboard, achieving a variety of images and a sense of continuity by using the full frames, then zooming in for close-ups and details. This is obviously much cheaper than a fully animated animatic. Usually, however, the studio will produce a single background, or a series of backgrounds, and cut-outs of all the individual components, including animals, figures and furniture – in many ways the process resembles the creation of a child's cardboard theatre. To give more flexibility figures are often drawn with moving parts, or with several alternative arm, leg and head positions, so that a variety of attitudes and positions can be set up against the background. So, instead of drawing the frames for a storyboard, each frame is set up and photographed on a rostrum camera. When completed, the film gives an illusion of movement. Because there are fewer frames per second the result is cruder than proper animation, but despite the jerky movements these little films are remarkably effective and have a special charm of their own.

Sometimes studios work on video first. The background is laid out on a light box, the moving elements are assembled on the background, then the frames that make up each sequence are videoed – this allows them to experiment with particular effects and different arrangements of the pieces, and to produce a rough animatic. This is sometimes shown to the client so that the studio can assess their reactions before incurring the expense of producing a complete animatic.

The final animatic is drawn on layout paper, the moving elements double-mounted to give them added strength and opacity. The cut edges of the moving pieces are coloured with brushpen so that the white does not show.

An animatic might be commissioned by a client in order to test whether a proposed commercial will show the product in the best light, convey the message successfully and reach the target audience. They might use it for market reasearch, for example.

They are also commissoned by advertising agencies who want to impress a new, and potentially valuable, client – if they don't get the contract the production costs will have to be written off! Originally, animatics were compiled by filming storyboards – by moving from frame to frame, overshooting, zooming in and moving out, the producer created the illusion of movement. Gradually the artists, designers and production companies became more ambitious and introduced increasingly complex effects. Clients and agencies began to expect and demand these ambitious results. Inevitably, the cost of the average animatic crept up, until they were almost as sophisticated as many full animations – and nearly as costly. As the prices have soared there is now a swing back to simpler, less ambitious animatics.

Studio: Presentation Video
Artist: Rob McCaig

In the first picture we show some of the elements used for an animatic of a man getting out of bed.

In the pictures on this page we have assembled the separate pieces in front of the camera to show how some of the effects were produced. However, on the printed page it is impossible to show the effects that can be achieved on film. We have deliberately allowed the joins to show so that you can see how the pieces fit – in the actual animatic great care was taken to make sure that the pieces fitted exactly, thereby reducing the differences between each shot and producing a fluid series of actions.

The artist was supplied with a very slight brief – a few scamps, a script and some stick-men drawings. From these he worked up pencil roughs which were shown to the art director and copy writer. When the concept was approved the artist set to work on the visuals. He used Magic Markers on an A3 Letraset marker pad. The flesh tones preferred by this artist are Powder Pink, Sand, Brick White, Orientale and a selection of Warm and Cool Greys. He finds this range more useful than the Blush and Flesh colours which produce too pink a tone.

This is a very simple animatic – the background of the room, the bed and the man's torso are all static pieces. The moving parts were treated as separate segments. The drawing is direct, with the marker colour applied boldly and tonal contrasts both simplified and exaggerated to maximize impact. The main frame was mounted up on a copyboard in front of a rostrum camera and shot. The second frame was mounted and shot. Then the two were overlapped and shot together – this softens the action. After shooting the third frame, the second shot was overlapped with the third and so on.

Studio: Helicopter
Artist: Carol Millard

It is very difficult to demonstrate exactly how effective animatics can be, for they are a moving medium, and their impact depends not only on the skill with which they are designed and drawn, but also on the skill of the art director and the production company. We asked Carol Millard to produce the artwork for a simple animatic, so that we could show how some of the effects are achieved.

Above, we show the background used for this simple animatic of a man mowing a lawn. The artist used fineliner for the line work, and a selection of markers were used to fill in these outlines with flat, matt colour. The only texture was reserved for the timber of the fence and the hut which was rendered very simply with Buttercup Yellow, Sand and Light Suntan.

Above, we show the elements used for the man pushing the mower, mopping his brow and turning his head. There are two leg, two head and two hand positions. The background was rendered on bleedproof marker paper, the moving parts were drawn on layout paper and double-mounted. They were then cut out, and the edges darkened with a brushpen.

The sequence of four pictures above has been assembled from the separate elements. We have photographed it so that you can see the acetate overlay. On the animatic the producer would have the opportunity to crop into some of the frames. Here, you can see the man progress from left to right, mopping his brow and turning his head as he goes.

Right, the man is given another set of legs.

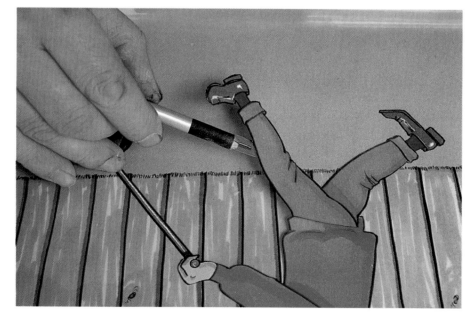

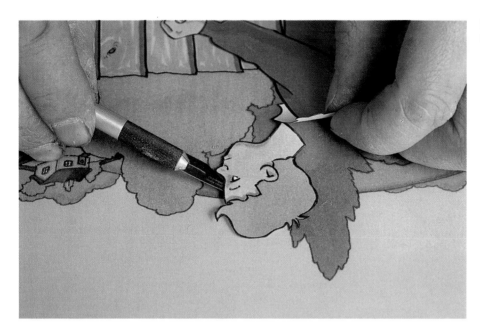

Left, the first head is carefully removed, ready for the next stage (below).

Left, another head is slipped in. Make sure that the joining sections – here the neck – allow enough overlap to give a neat join.

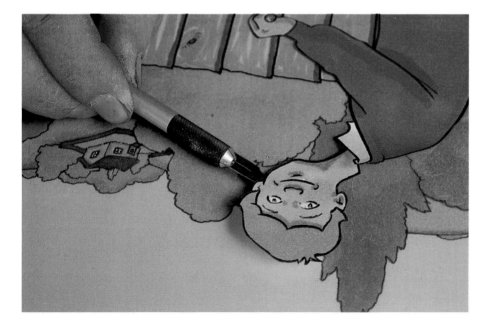

Slick or highly-finished

For the visualizer, style is important. Some artists specialize in one type of drawing, whilst others have a range of styles at their fingertips, and will frequently, if the job requires it, mix them. Clients often ask for a particular style of drawing, and may even specify which artist they want to do the work. The 'look' of the finished visual is just as important as its accuracy, the skill with which it is rendered, and the quality of the drawing.

Most of the work produced by visualizers in the advertising business can be grouped into four broad categories: slick, cartoon, realistic/highly finished and graphic. Naming the categories is easy, but defining the parameters and actually pigeonholing a particular piece of work is more difficult. What one artist or studio describes as highly finished would be classified as slick in another studio, and vice versa. As part of our research for this book we asked each studio for clarification, and were given increasingly contradictory definitions, especially for the term 'slick'. By far the best, but least helpful, was 'either you can see it or you can't'.

Slick is a style which seems particularly at home in the advertising environment, combining, as it does, quality with speed. Slick visuals are loose, good, but quickly produced. They are full of technique and combine limited use of tone with simple colour. The images are, however, realistically and descriptively rendered, with clean, sharp lines and minimal detail. Movement is often depicted with speed lines. In many ways the style resembles the very best sci-fi comic illustrations. Slick is definitely one of the hardest styles to tie down, but basically it allows the artist to produce a job which looks good, in a hurry.

Highly finished work is often requested by clients. Whilst most good marker artists could produce a highly finished visual given the time, a few specialize in producing this type of work. In highly finished visuals the line work is not usually obvious and is used to define details rather than outlines. The aim is an almost photographic realism because the final product will be either a photograph or film. A lot of detail will be included, so on close inspection it will be possible to see the pitted surface of an orange, or the texture of hair, or the eyes, eyelashes and teeth of a model. To achieve this degree of finish takes time. The artist develops the image gradually, tightening up the details, often introducing other media, such as gouache, non-bleed white, pastel, chalk and coloured pencil. Brushes and pencils allow the artist

Artist: Gareth Pitman

This energetic drawing relies for its impact on the composition: the way the image fills the picture area, and the strong diagonal of the figure which leads the eye over the subject. The artist used a black fineliner for the outline and linework, then laid in the body of the rider and the mudguards with Cadmium Orange and Red, with various Cool **Greys for the shadows on the figure and for the spatters of mud. He used Cadmium Orange, Pale Blue, Manganese Blue and a little Prussian Blue for the vizor and the Honda sign on the jacket. The white of the paper provides the highlights, and folds and creases in the rider's suit are drawn in with fineliner. The tyres and the engine were laid in with a combination of Cool Greys and Black.**

Artist: Harry Bloom

Studio: Storyboard Harpers
Artist: John White

This example crosses the line between slick and highly finished. The artist uses the white of the paper for the highlights, building up layers of colour to create the dark tones.

This accomplished and atmospheric visual was created using a very small range of colours. The artist has used an Impressionistic technique, laying down slashes of broken colour which combine in the eye, rather than blending on the paper. The colours are seen as quite discrete patches close to, but from a distance combine to create a convincing illusion of dappled sunlight in a woodland scene.

Agency: Ogilvy & Mather
Studio: Storyboard Harpers
Artist: Joe Lawrence
Client: Imperial Tobacco

Here, airbrush and marker have been combined to create a highly realistic representation of a stained glass craftsman at work. The brief for the project was quite specific and the artist and studio had to make an intensive study of the methods, techniques and materials of stained glass making before they could start work. They found out what tools were used, collected photographic reference and used samples of stained glass work to ensure that the visual was as accurate and realistic as possible. The stipples in the green glass were created by dabbing with a bullet-tipped pen, whilst the streaks in the orange glass were made by laying lines of marker over solid colour. Whilst the artist has achieved a high degree of finish, the techniques he has used are very simple.

to achieve finer details than would be possible with the studio marker, which is rather a blunt drawing instrument. Obviously this type of work is expensive, reflecting the time and effort involved.

Visuals about food are usually highly finished for the product must always look appetizing, it must have 'food appeal'. Some artists specialize not only in a particular degree of finish but in certain subjects. Thus, one will be particularly adept at capturing the human figure and another will deal with food subjects, whilst another will deal with pack shots.

Artist: David Lee

The artist specializes in highly finished work. He started by laying in a very light outline with watercolour and a fine sable brush. He then mixed a middle flesh tone with gouache paint, and with this laid in the dark tones around the nose, cheeks and jawline.

Watercolour and brush allows him to achieve a softer, subtler blending of tones than is possible with marker. With the outline and these important dark tones established, he then started to fill in the main colour areas. He used Cool Greys, Pale Blue and Black for the dress, and the flesh tones were laid in with Brick White, Powder Pink and

Pale Rose. In some places the paper shows through as white highlights — on the inside of the arm for example. In others thinly diluted white gouache provides highlights. The artist added final touches with gouache and a fine sable brush — redefining the outline, adding details to the eyes and dark tones to the hair.

Studio: Storyboard Harpers
Artist: Derek Watson

This sample rough was produced for the artist's portfolio. He specializes in rather mechanical subjects which require a knowledge of technical drawing. For this piece the artist worked on quite a large scale – using an A3 sheet of bleedproof marker paper. A Pentel fineliner was used for the outline and details, and the basic colours were then laid in with Magic Marker. He left the white of the paper to stand for the highlights on the top surfaces of the boat and for the broken water in the wake.

Agency: Ogilvy & Mather
Studio: Storyboard Harpers
Artist: David Lee
Client: Beecham Foods (Beechams, Beecham)

This is the last frame of a storyboard for a commercial. The artist specializes in this type of accurately rendered, very highly finished work. He does a rough work-out with black felt pen or marker, and then uses this as a trace for the final visual. He lays in the outlines with paint and a brush, which gives the drawing a soft, rather fluid feeling. He then lays in the colour with Magic Marker, using the gutted marker for large areas such as the background. The dark tones are built up gradually as layers of colour. He adds highlights in white paint at the very end. He has used a mixture of white and yellow gouache on the chair and the man's shirt, and pure white paint for the dog's white coat.

Cartoon

Some visuals demand a humorous, jokey, or light-hearted approach, but humour is difficult to categorize and what one person finds amusing will fail to raise even a smile in another. Nevertheless, many advertisers use humour in their commercials and advertisements, and the visualizer must be able to capture this quality. Perhaps the simplest example of this is when the final product is an animation featuring cartoon characters. If the characters are already established, the artist will have to become familiar with their appearance and characteristics in order to reproduce them. This type of drawing often consists of an outline infilled with flat colour, an application ideally suited to marker for it is easy (with a little practice) to lay areas of flat colour.

The visualizer may be required to depict an amusing situation or character, and there are various ways of introducing humour into a visual. An element of caricature is usually involved, but humour can also be expressed in the quality of the outline and the way colour is used. Most cartoon-style visuals use an outline drawing which may be very stylized. The line may be spiky, rounded or exaggerated in some way – the figures may all be slightly elongated, for example. Colour too may be applied in a variety of ways, it may be flat, scribbled, simplified or rather personal. Again, artists tend to specialize in this type of work.

Artist: Paul Langford

Here, the word Booths is transformed into frames for sunglasses. The visual is obviously lighthearted, and the artist has used a simple brushpen outline on marker paper. The faces are described with great economy – a mid skin-tone is applied first, leaving white patches of paper for the highlights. Then the darkest tones are applied with briskly applied strokes of colour which follow form. On the right-hand picture the artist has used pink gouache to

Studio: Drawers

One of a series of concept boards presented to a client as part of a biscuit campaign, this is an excellent example of a slick visual. The artist worked on quite a large scale, on A2 marker paper, but his skill as a draughtsman and his fast, loose technique allowed him to develop the image quickly. The spiky outline and details were drawn in black fineliner, and the colour was then applied with Magic Marker, working from light to dark and allowing the white of the paper to stand for highlights.

create the fizzy effect and white for the gleam on the spectacles.

Studio: Drawers

The drawing below was part of a series of concept boards for an advertisement. The artist has caricatured the women to make the humour of the situation more apparent. The drawing is free and rather spiky, and is executed with a black fineliner. The marker colour is freely and loosely applied, the white of the paper showing through in places, on the arm and face of the nearest woman, for example, where it stands for the lightest flesh tones. The freedom of the rendering leaves the art director plenty of scope for his own input.

Artist: Paul Langford

Here, the artist has used caricature, distortion and vivid colours to create a dramatic cartoon. He drew directly onto marker paper with a hard pencil – soft pencil blotches and spreads if marker is applied over it. He then went over the outlines with a black brushpen, which gives a softer, more fluid line than fineliner. He used a waterbased brushpen, as a spirit-based ink would bleed into the marker. Before adding the colour he soaked a tissue with lighter fuel and applied this to the paper to diffuse the marker, creating a softer effect.

Graphic

In this style the image is simplified by using flat colour, simple outlines and little or no tone. Thus, the abstract qualities of the composition are emphasized, creating a dramatic image. This highly stylized approach has great impact and is colourful and attractive. Many artists include this approach in their repertoire and it is sometimes requested by clients, though it tends to be more appropriate for some applications rather than others. It is, for example, quite often used in connection with fashion products and products with a high design profile, but rarely for food where a more realistic approach is called for. This style seems to go in and out of fashion more than any other.

Marker is ideal for a graphic approach, for, used correctly, it is possible to lay areas of completely flat colour in a way that is impossible with any other medium. Also, the bright, vibrant range of colours lends itself to this treatment.

Studio: Drawers

In the dramatic drawing (left) marker has been used primarily for its vivid colours, rather than for its ability to render tone and form. If the colour is applied briskly, it will have virtually no modulations of tone, and will resemble the flatness which can be achieved in the printing process. The black outline of the broad forms was laid in with a fineliner and the artist then filled in the colour areas. By flattening the forms the artist draws attention to the abstract, pattern-making qualities of the subject.

Studio: Storyboard Harpers
Artist: Harry Bloom

The drawing at the top of this page is a key frame from a concept board. It shows the proposed style and treatment of characters and background. The starkness of the images, the elongation and stylization of the characters, and the simple but strong palette give this image enormous impact. Again, the artist uses outline and flat colour with little tonal variation, creating pattern rather than form.

Artist: Harry Bloom

Here, flat colour and simplified forms are used to dramatic effect. The artist has exploited an absorbent surface, allowing the marker to bleed at the edges to soften the outline. He creates crisp edges for the highlight areas by cutting them away with a sharp blade, allowing the white paper beneath to show through.

Rendering food

Images of food figure large in our visual world – on television, in magazines, on hoardings and on the packaging in supermarkets – almost everywhere you look there are luscious and seductive morsels tempting our palette and our pocket. What this tells us is that food, and the advertising of it, is big business. Manufacturers spend vast amounts of money persuading us to indulge in their latest offering or to stay with an existing product. Interestingly, the food industry no longer commands the market in the way it once did, as brands have given way to the big retailers. Other areas now loom large in the accounts of the major agencies – the financial market has recently crept into a leading position from almost nowhere a few years ago.

Nevertheless, the cost of launching a new product or promoting an old one is so high that the client must be quite sure of the effectiveness of the message before he will commit himself. A great deal of consumer research is done – manufacturers often use an animatic rendered in marker as part of their market research. £8,000-£10,000 spent on an animatic to test response to a particular campaign will be a drop in the ocean compared to the £1-2 million spent on the television commercial.

This is where the marker artist comes in. The agency will present the client with a series of proposals, and in order to give each the best possible chance they spend a great deal of time, effort and money making sure that the presentation has maximum impact. The marker artist may be asked to prepare several types of material, such as finished visuals, storyboards, or animatics. These will have to be prepared quickly, and it is essential that they have 'meal appeal'. Food visuals present the artist with particular problems, and not every artist is capable of meeting the challenge. The product must look attractive, appetizing and realistic, so the work tends to go to those artists who have a fairly tight, realistic style. A slice of roast pork must look like roast pork, not luncheon meat. The products must look fresh

Agency: McCann Erikson Advertising Ltd
Studio: Storyboard Harpers
Artist: Kevin Seale/Derek Walston
Client: Del Monte

Marker is a particularly appropriate medium for dealing with this vivid and colourful subject. This frame from a fruit juice animatic is designed to show the fresh, natural and healthy ingredients used in the product. The artist used a combination of marker, bullet-tipped pen and white paint, applying the colour freely and matching the method of application to the subject. Thus in the background the colour is applied broadly at first, then more descriptive marks are used for the pattern of the foliage. The pitted skins of the oranges and lemons are built up using a stippling technique, whilst for the flesh of the fruit he uses a dark yellow bullet-tipped pen over pale yellow marker. The white highlights are gouache applied with a sable brush. The artist's approach is direct – he has analyzed and simplified the subject and found a simple but effective shorthand for the textures. He has dispensed with outline in order to give the image a softer and more natural feel.

without looking garish. Texture is obviously important – a lettuce leaf must look crisp and fresh, a slice of bread must look soft inside, crusty on the outside. The artists who handle this sort of work know what the client is looking for, and develop a formula for achieving particular results. They will almost always work from some sort of reference. This can be a photograph or the actual product. Colour is important. On packaging, for example, greens tend to be avoided on all but naturally green products – on anything but a lettuce or a cabbage green implies mould. Blues, on the other hand, are cool and clean and are associated with sparkling mineral water, yogurt and branded milks.

Studio: Drawers

Here, the artist has used a much tighter technique. He combines marker with a finepoint which he uses for the initial drawing and for details such as the ribbing on the celery and onions in the sauce. The detail reveals his approach. The complex mesh of the pasta is drawn in with a finepoint. He then blocks in the pale green of the tagliatelli, working quickly and keeping the front edge wet. He establishes the darkest tones with a dark warm grey, then uses a lighter warm grey for the mid-tones. The speckles of herbs are dabbed in with marker and sharpened up with a brushpen. Highlights are touched in with white gouache, and steam rising from the dish is suggested by a smear of powdered pastel applied with a finger. The artist knows his subject and his medium, and is able to create an image which is realistic, but not overworked.

Figure and portrait rendering

The ability to produce convincing drawings of the human form eludes some of the most accomplished artists. To draw the figure well the artist must first understand the way it works, and this understanding can only be gained by drawing from life. The artist must draw from the figure repeatedly, working from different angles, and constantly changing the pose so that he or she draws from the model in repose as well as from the moving figure. A knowledge of anatomy helps, though some very good figure artists profess only a sketchy knowledge of what goes on under the skin. Some people will never be able to cope convincingly with the human figure: no matter how hard they apply themselves, their figures will always look wooden and contrived. Others have a natural flair which allows them to depict any figure from any angle without reference. This facility is not common — those that have it are in great demand, and can often command a premium for their work. They tend to specialize in figure work, not necessarily from choice but because that is what they are asked to do most often.

Drawing the head demands many of the same skills, though here the artist is also required to achieve a likeness. The brief may be very specific — for example, to produce a portrait of a well-known personality. Alternatively, it may not be a particular individual but a type which is required, such as a five-year-old child or a 45-year-old woman.

Studio: Drawers
Artist: Sue Hilda

This highly stylized approach uses a coloured pencil outline, flat marker colour and areas of texture applied with coloured pencil. Basic skin tones are built up using only two shades of marker. The white of the paper represents the highlights and brown pencil the darkest tones.

Artist: Garth Pitman

Left: the artist has used a range of markers to render the lights and darks which give form to the head. When viewed close-to, the free handling of the marker is apparent, yet when seen from a distance the tones blend into one another, creating an illusion of form.

Studio: Drawers

Right: the artist has used a combination of loosely applied marker colour and vigorous line-work to create a slick, succinct image. The figure is attractive and stylish, and the artist's obvious knowledge of the subject gives the image an apparent ease — the work of a less accomplished artist would have been more laboured.

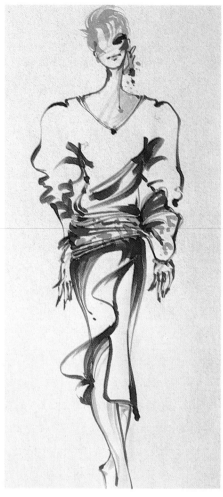

Studio: Drawers

The entire picture was rendered in brushpen, a medium which this artist has made especially her own. The sinuous lines and brilliant colours make for an elegant, rather stylized image. Her style is particularly suited to fashion work.

Studio: Storyboard Harpers

Above: the brief was to demonstrate the continuity of a product by setting an obviously contemporary man against a dated background, so the background elements are as important as the foreground figure. The artist has used a variety of techniques to give the key objects solidity and presence. The image of the man is realistic, although the planes of the face have been rendered in a rather schematized way. Marker and felt pen have been used for the television, with stippled and hatched effects to describe different textures. The lampshade is drawn in marker, with the stitching applied in white paint at a later stage.

Artist: Garth Pitman

Above: the artist has achieved subtle gradations of skin tones by subtly blending the marker colours. He had to work very quickly to avoid hard edges, blocking in the broad forms with Brick White, and working into it with Beige and Light Suntan while still wet.

Studio: Drawers

Above: brushpen is used to create a lively image, the vigorous linework capturing the energy of the children and implying a sense of movement. The artist's expressive use of colour adds to the excitement and impact of the picture.

Artist: David Lee

Above: brush and paint outline, broad areas of colour laid down in marker; tones gradually built up as layers of colour; highlights in paint.

Collaboration

Marker visuals are often composed of separate pieces which are only brought together at a late stage. The background, for example, may be treated as a single continuous element and blocked in quickly with a giant marker, a gutted marker or even an airbrush. The foreground, figures etc are then drawn up separately and coloured in; the artist can work quickly and freely because the outline can be disregarded. When colouring is finished, the foreground and other elements are cut out with a knife and assembled on the background. Because marker paper is so thin, it is only by inspecting the artwork closely that you can tell whether it is all of a piece or a composite.

One of the ways in which studios manage to produce high-quality visuals very quickly is by putting two, or possibly three, artists onto a job. Animatics and storyboards, in particular, are often handled in this way for they usually involve several separate pieces of artwork that maintain continuity from frame to frame. In order to turn the job round in a matter of hours the studio manager will allocate the work to different artists: one may concentrate on the background, another on the foreground and yet another on the figures. All the frames are sketched out first, then each artist works on their section and the separate elements are assembled at the end. By distributing the work in this way visuals can be produced much faster than is possible if a single individual does all the work, continuity is maintained from frame to frame, and artists can be used for the subjcts they are particularly good at — for figures or motor cars, for example.

Agency: Yellowhammer
Artist: Chris Mynheer
Client: Mitsubishi

Below: the background is airbrush on CS10, the car is Magic Marker and Caran d'Ache aquarelle pencil on non-bleed marker paper. The artist made a drawing of the car then, placing this under the marker paper, started to work up the image in marker.

Studio: L'Image
Artist: Chris Mynheer
Client: Powis Game Shoot

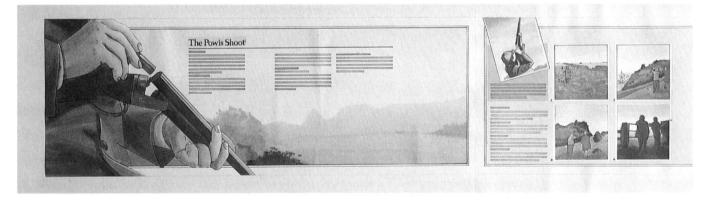

The background was washed in with a gutted marker applied to lighter fuel-wetted paper. The misty effect was created by airbrushing white paint over the marker colour. For the man loading a gun, the artist used marker for the broad forms, picking out details with black waterbased fineliner.

Studio: Drawers

This frame from an animatic (above) is the work of three artists, divided as follows: background; figurework and fishing equipment; trees, river and foreground. Magic Marker was used for most of the colourwork, fineliner for outlines and details, and pastels and white gouache for the lighter tones, highlights and for the halo of brightness around the clouds. If you look carefully at the detail (left) you can see the cut edges of the trees.

In the world of film and video the ability to visualize ideas quickly, efficiently and imaginatively is highly valued. As in advertising, the artist works closely with a team of people, gathering, interpreting and expressing their ideas in order that they can be evaluated, and then used by others in the production process. There are two main areas for the application of marker: in film storyboards, which visualize a script or an idea sequence by sequence, and poster roughs.

Posters

Producing posters for the film industry is a demanding activity and some studios specialize in that area exclusively. A film poster has a difficult job of work to do. It has to succeed in a variety of locations and often in several countries, though distributors will sometimes change posters in response to particular national requirements. The poster must, for example, be effective when viewed from across the line in a subway station, but must also work when seen close-up on the platform wall. It must encapsulate the spirit of the film, whilst emphasizing what the distributors see as its main audience-pulling features. It must also draw in the right audience—those of a nervous disposition should not mistakenly find themselves at a horror movie, whilst a vehicle for a pop star should attract a predominantly youthful audience.

The designer and artist are usually faced with several, often conflicting, interests. They must reconcile the commercial requirements of the distributors, the artistic intentions of the director, and their own perception of what is appropriate. There are also practical considerations to be borne in mind. The images must be used in such a way that the typographic elements can be accommodated comfortably—the viewer must be able to pick out important pieces of information at a glance. The name of the film, the director and the

Studio: Feref Associates
Artist: Brian Bysouth

For the *A Passage to India* poster the artist worked from an A2 black and white sketch. This was PMT'd up to A1 to break up the line. The hard, non-absorbent surface of the photographic paper causes the marker ink to sit on the surface and slows drying, allowing the artist to blend colours and create washes. He completes the drawing by spraying it with fixative. The droplets of fix react with the marker, forming pools of colour which dry with crisp edges. These break up the colour areas and give the drawing an unusual brilliance and sparkle. A similar effect can be achieved by working on tracing paper, but you sacrifice the whiteness of the support. The technique is simple and effective, but timing is important and only with practice will you learn just when fix should be applied and in what quantities.

DAVID LEAN'S FILM OF E.M. FORSTER'S
A PASSAGE TO INDIA

major stars must be displayed prominently, venues and dates must be legible, and easy to find, but other information may not need the same emphasis. A further complication is that in the United Kingdom poster display boards outside cinemas have a landscape format, whilst elsewhere in the world a portrait format is used. This generally means that two versions of the artwork must be produced, so it is important that the design which is chosen is effective in both forms.

All these potential problems should be sorted out at the briefing between client, art director and artist. Once an 'angle' has been decided on, the visualizer develops the ideas working from the script and stills – if he is lucky, he will also have seen the film. Generally, these first ideas are sketched out in pencil – this looks more tentative than other media, and the client feels freer to make changes. If these first roughs are approved the artist then works up colour visuals. If these in turn meet with approval they will be used as a basis for the final artwork, which may be a gouache illustration, or a photograph.

A visual for the film *Highlander*, produced in landscape format for Britain and portrait format for the rest of the world. Brian Bysouth started with an outline drawing, then PMT'd it onto photographic paper. The lighter tones were laid in first: reds and yellows for the flesh and a pale blue for the background. He gradually built up the darker tones with layers of colour. The colour dries slowly on photographic paper so he had to be careful not to overwork the image, and allow each layer to dry off a little before applying another. The streaky effect, created by using marker on this non-absorbent surface, is a particularly attractive feature of the visual. Finally, he applied a fine spray of fixative over the whole image, then sprayed another layer around the edges, holding the nozzle so as to create larger droplets in some areas. The fixative combines with the marker ink to create the crackled effect which adds sparkle to the image.

Storyboards for film

Film-making is a very complex business. A director has to orchestrate the activities of various artists and technicians during the production process, so he needs a visual synopsis to which everyone can refer. Hence, the storyboard (sometimes referred to as the 'shootboard') is an integral part of film production. Produced by a commissioned artist, it is a frame-by-frame visual interpretation of the script, which provides a broad, not too rigid framework for the project, and leaves plenty of scope for reinterpretation, editing and creativity later on. In some films every frame is drawn before shooting, but usually the board is restricted to action or special-effects scenes—where, given the costs involved, advance planning is most important. Producing a storyboard can take anything from a few months to 3 years, and often involves thousands of drawings. Throughout, the artist works closely with art, props and costume departments, location photos etc, to ensure that the various components of a scene are accurately related to each other, and to the various camera positions. By the time filming starts, the boards will be heavily annotated with notes for the director, camera crew etc, so the storyboard artist will require, in addition to the usual skills, a working knowledge of film procedures.

Artist: Martin Asbury
Client: Warner Bros.

This sequence of storyboard sketches, below and opposite, is a small but energetic fragment of the 3500 drawn for the Warner Bros. film, Greystoke. Because storyboards are an important reference for those making a film they must be informative, but they should also excite, and trigger ideas. The energy of this sequence stems from a calligraphic use of fineliners, contrasted with bold tonal effects. The Letraset paper is sprayed with lighter fuel to turn marker strokes into washes, and wax crayons, gouache and pencils are used to highlight the important action.

(27)   EXT. FOREST . CLAYTON STALKING .

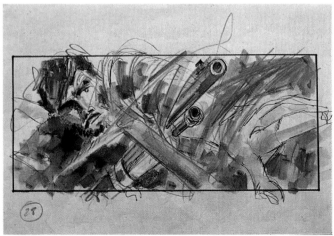

Concept boards for video

Concept boards are usually commissioned by the video production agency. As the main purpose is to sell a concept to the client, and because clients tend to have a limited visual sense, the boards are slick, highly finished presentation drawings – utilizing all the tricks of marker rendering. Again, the artist must be capable of visualizing and drawing quickly and skilfully from the written word and the often obscure desires of the agency producer.

Because concept boards are drawn before shooting starts, the artist can find himself, albeit temporarily, acting as director, art director and casting director for the whole project. He has a real opportunity to input ideas and set the style. However, by the time the concept board has been discussed and dissected by the client and the agency, then the final video may well bear little relationship to the original presentation. Nevertheless, concept boards are often used by the director as 'working drawings' during production.

Studio: Animation City
Artist: Phil Austin
Client: Spandau Ballet

This sequence of concept boards is interesting because the artist's starting point was the client's finishing point: Animation City were handed an LP sleeve design from which to produce a TV advertisement. The commercial had to finish with a shot of the new album cover, so the artist decided to work backwards from this to conceive the film.

At the outset a number of ideas were explored. The darkroom theme was chosen to be developed further into concept boards – using markers and a Frisk storyboard pad. Picture 1 shows the first board of the completed sequence. A simple outline was drawn using a fibre-tip, then the colours were blocked in with Magic Markers. The nuance of reds and oranges expressed the atmosphere of darkroom lighting. Note the method of utilizing the white paper to represent light – a traditional watercolour technique now used in a modern medium.

The proposed commercial used a combination of animated and live action sequences, and the artwork for the animation mock-up, and for the final shoot, was based closely on these concept boards – typed labels were attached to the boards to carry proposed production information and ideas. (In fact the stylized enlarger, shown in picture 1, was turned into three dimensions for the animation.)

As the sequence developed, and the band emerged as the focal point, more details were put in with fineliners. And picture 6 shows how one rectangle offset inside another was used to create movement and impact. Colour also serves a purpose – the sudden use of cool colours in frame 7 changes the mood completely, and grabs the viewer's attention.

There is a continuity of style and an inventive use of simple methods throughout this sequence. Note the penultimate board shares similarities of colour and composition with the first board. This type of link is an effective method of unifying the storyboard visually and conceptually.

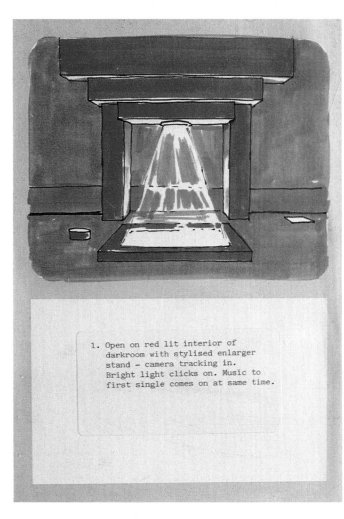

1. Open on red lit interior of darkroom with stylised enlarger stand – camera tracking in. Bright light clicks on. Music to first single comes on at same time.

3. As we close in we see still of band under enlarger.

3. An still comes into close-up light and music click off and band disappears.

4. Match cut to developing tank, video starts to dissolve through underneath the developer.

Music to second single mixes in.

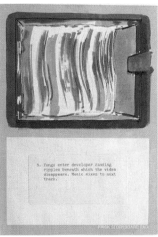

5. Tongs enter developer sending ripples beneath which the video disappears. Music mixes to next track.

6. Boxing video held in tongs is lifted up.

7. Video comes full frame.

8. Video freezes on close-up and guillotine trims photo. Music to third single is cut off.

9. Photo moves back onto drying line Music to 4th single comes in.

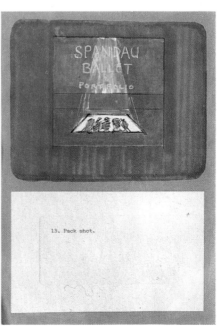

10. Pan along drying line.

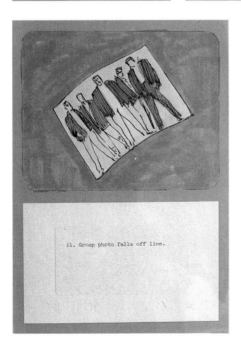

11. Group photo falls off line.

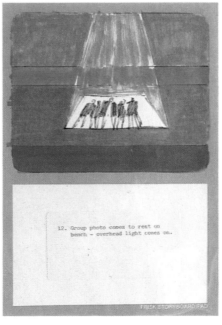

12. Group photo comes to rest on bench - overhead light comes on.

13. Pack shot.

6 Packaging

Packaging is enormously important to the success of a product, since at the point of sale – that is, on the supermarket shelf or the counter display – the package is what gets the product noticed. Even the best-designed product may not sell if the packaging is boring or inappropriate. Packaging can even make the buyer choose the more expensive of two alternatives, since a good pack invests a product with an air of quality or freshness that makes it more attractive.

What makes a package attractive?

In most cases, the buyer's eye is drawn to a pack by a striking design in bold colours. This also applies, of course, to the artist's rough visual for the package, which has to appeal to the client. The boldness and brightness of marker makes it an ideal tool for this purpose. Not surprisingly, most packaging visuals are done wholly or partly in this medium.

Cigarette packs are a well-known example of the importance of a distinctive colour. By the end of the 1950s most British packs had become almost identical. They were copies of the leading American brands: white or almost white, with restrained lettering and some small ornament such as an imitation coat of arms. In the United Kingdom cigarettes were usually displayed in rows on small shelves behind the counter, so that they were quite a long way from the buyer's eye. Because a cigarette packet is a small object it was really very hard to tell which brand was which, and there was certainly no incentive to try a new brand. (This was before the days of supermarket displays in Britain, but a display of nearly identical small packets on an American supermarket shelf would have been equally monotonous and confusing.)

The first brand to break out of the rut was called Mayfair. It had a pack that was bright red all over, so it really stood out from the others on the shelf. To make it even more noticeable, it was advertised as 'Mayfair in the red, red box' – a slogan which had nothing to do with the quality of the cigarettes, but nevertheless sold it.

Of course, other manufacturers rushed in to copy Mayfair's example, and the supply of bright colours soon became exhausted. Current examples of successful attempts to look different are the gold Benson and Hedges and the black Players' packs – both of which are also advertised on the basis of the colour (though this is partly due to the fact that advertisers aren't allowed to mention much else in cigarette advertisements).

Studio: Michael Peters Group

For this visual of a German nut pack the artist worked on Daler layout paper. Magic Marker was used for the gradated background as well as for the subject. Many artists prefer to combine airbrush gradation with marker to create this type of effect.

Packaging artists

Because of the enormous importance of packaging, and the constant demand for new pack designs, packaging artists are usually specialists, designing nothing else. In fact, they often specialize even more narrowly than that. One artist may concentrate on pictures of food and another on backgrounds, and they may collaborate to produce a rough visual or a finished design.

When a new product is designed, the packaging artist will consult its designer with a view to displaying the product in the most effective way.

Marker is used for rough visuals to show to clients, but when a design has been selected the marker drawing suffers the usual fate of marker drawings (ie, it is binned) and the final design is almost always done in other, more precise media.

Displaying the product

With many products, especially food, the buyer wants to see what he or she is getting. Of course, it is possible to have a transparent pack or one with a window; but often the food, although perfectly wholesome, looks rather unprepossessing. The solution is to use a picture of the food on the pack. Food illustration is one of the most important fields of packaging, and one of the most difficult to get right. Whether a photograph, a painting or a drawing is used, the borderline between what appears appetizing and what looks disgusting is very small. Many foods photograph badly—ice cream tends to look like half-melted lard—and great skill and a certain amount of trickery are necessary to get good results. Therefore a drawing or painting is often preferred.

Studio: Michael Peters Group
Client: Boots the Chemist

The brief for the design shown right was to create a pack that promoted the healthy, good quality aspects of the product. Pale Yellow Magic Marker was used to render the olive oil, with additional layers in places to create the shading and tonal effect. The lettering—part hand-drawn, part typeset—was made into a transfer and stuck on.

35·2 floz 1litre

Pure Olive Oil

Good faces, either human or type,
try to use only the typefaces which are character.

Studio: Michael Peters Group

For this visual the artist used a blue bullet-tipped pen on detail paper to create the effect of printing on a plastic bag, and a hatching technique, like that of an old engraving, to invest the image with nostalgia.

The power of association

The three visuals on these pages are all trying to do much the same thing: to sell seafood. In the first case, the scampi packet, a picture of the food itself would be hardly appropriate. A Dublin Bay prawn is a spidery and rather alarming-looking creature. If it was shown peeled, the effect would be even worse. So the alternatives are a 'serving suggestion' picture, showing the scampi decently clothed in batter against a background of attractive foods; or this romantic and nostalgic image in which the scampi plays only a minor role.

The fact that scampi are not caught by picturesque old fishermen in rowing boats, and that if the buyer thought for a moment, the whole scene would be revealed as a fraud, doesn't matter. The associations of freshness, tradition, and honest toil are what matter. In fact, people unthinkingly buy all kinds of 'traditional' or 'country-style' foods made by modern processes in modern factories. What they are choosing is not the food but the idea.

The second picture also uses a romantic fishing scene, but a more realistic and up-to-date one, which might even resemble a Mediterranean mussel-gathering enterprise. But mussel shells are quite handsome objects, so here it is possible to have them in the foreground, attractively displayed in a traditional basket, to reinforce the idea of natural goodness.

The third visual uses the high-risk strategy of presenting the product on its own. The artist has clearly enjoyed the interesting shape and inviting pink colour of the newly cooked prawns, made more appetizing by a hint of steam. The only added association is that perhaps the name flag suggests a good old-fashioned fishmonger's slab. But in the last analysis the appeal of the packet depends on the buyer liking the look of the whiskery little things.

Here, the product plays a greater role in the image. An artist put in the background with Magic Markers, on the reverse side of the paper. The pale tones and pastel effect was achieved by modifying the marker strokes with petrol. A second artist drew the mussels on the front of the sheet, using black felt-tipped pens and markers.

This visual is known as a positioning concept. The product is presented in unadulterated glory. The artist drew this dynamic pattern with markers. The attention-grabbing eyes, and the subtle wisps of steam, were added with crayons. Marker was used to drop in the trompe-l'oeil shadow around the white name flag.

Placing the product in the market

These two visuals use associations more subtly than the designs on pages 96–7. Both were produced as part of a set of widely different designs, each intended to appeal to a different type of buyer. The coffee pack set included not only this jazzy, 'young' carnival design but more staid ones (Glen Tutsell, a director of the Michael Peters Group, called them 'cup-and-saucer' images) that were designed to give the idea of friends dropping in for a cup of coffee, a biscuit and a chat.

The wine box design is for Californian wine, which normally has an up-market, expensive image. Other designs in the set projected an idea of high quality. However, the wine itself was an inexpensive one, and so this design was created to give a no-nonsense effect. It's still clearly marked 'Californian'—a selling point—and there is a picture of the Golden Gate Bridge to reinforce this. But the deliberately workaday brown paper and the stencilled 'packing case' lettering convey unpretentiousness (paradoxically, because it isn't a real stencil and the brown paper effect would have to be printed). Note how the stencil effect is enhanced by the diagonal, overlapping lettering and the standard packing case symbols for 'fragile' and 'this side up'.

Studio: Michael Peters Group

This design, above, for packaging a new blend of coffee, was one of a number of alternatives presented to the client. Drawn with felt-tipped pens, the 'sun-filled' colour and lively graphics direct the product at the younger buyer. The quirky patterns convey a carnival atmosphere – pure Brazilian, like the coffee itself.

One of several visuals, left, produced to identify market area and product identity. This illustration is unashamedly utilitarian and therefore presents the product, wine, as 'genuine', having nothing to hide – as if straight from the cellar. To achieve the stencilled appearance the design was drawn up on white paper, lightly traced onto brown paper and then filled in with marker so that no outline could be seen.

Studio: Michael Peters Group

These striking designs are for the packaging of a new sweet. Prominent lettering means that pictorial content has to be succinct – fruits are drawn as symbols, and coloured with markers and felt-tips. Dry transfers were used for the lettering.

A set of alternatives

There isn't much room on a sweet wrapper. These visuals for a new Italian range of sweets are actual size, and most of the space is taken up by the large lettering – as it has to be if the product name is to be got across clearly.

Fruit-flavoured sweets have to project the idea of real fruit. These alternative designs, presented to the client, show how much variety is possible in putting across that idea in a small space. The lemons in 'Limone' are fruit machine symbols. The oranges in the two 'Arancia' designs are romantic, or zestfully squirting out flavour. The strawberries in the two 'Fragola' designs are reduced to symbols. 'Ciliege' shows one luscious black cherry. And the design for 'Menta' suggests the fresh taste of mint with a fizzy design of whirling stars and planets.

The brand name is in English because the Italians think English names are chic – just as the British use Italian names for cars. Also Britain has an overseas reputation for confectionery. Sometimes foreign manufacturers get English names splendidly wrong: there are Italian mint pastilles called 'Mental' and Norwegian fruit drops called 'Dropsy'.

Showing what the product does

'Before and after' pictures are as old as advertising itself: probably they were being scratched on walls in the cities of ancient Sumeria. Using them on a pack is a new and striking idea. Not surprisingly, the client liked it, and cans of wood colour using the design from this visual are now on sale in your local DIY shop. The rejected design of a loaded brush seems rather weak by comparison, though it also shows the effect of the product on wood.

The strength of these designs lies in their portrayal of the way that the products bring out the richness of the grain of wood. The effect is shown quite accurately, and the product as marketed has an appearance very similar to the visual shown here. The artist has cleverly exploited the fact that timber comes in planks to show the effect of the product on different kinds of wood, without reducing the boldness of the simple image.

Another good point of this design is that natural wood is a product associated with honesty and tradition. Even if the customer is buying a can printed in imitation of wood to apply to some real wood at home the association still works, in the same way that the spurious fisherman on the scampi packet (see page 96) conveys the idea that the frozen contents have come straight out of the sea.

And the design itself is extremely distinctive: a can that appears to be made of wood stands out strongly from the other, obviously metal, cans on the shelf. The dramatic, splattered zigzag of the brushmark also contrasts with the neat, tame graphics that are used on the majority of containers—especially for DIY products, a field not noted for good pack design.

Studio: Michael Peters Group

The illustration opposite is one from a number of concept designs, produced in close liaison with a market research department. At this stage no real attempt was made to show the curvature of the container – a simple outline was filled in with a base colour, using a pale marker. The woodgrain effect was achieved by letting the base tone break through the overlaid colours as a pale line. Above, the graduated background was put in with an airbrush using Magic Marker ink, and Magic Markers were used for the brush and to establish the woodgrain. The grain was finished, and shading added to the bristles, with crayons and felt-tipped pens. The design, right, was the one chosen for the product. Here, the woodgrain effect was drawn in with pale-toned markers. A second layer of marker colour was added to create the brushmark.

7 Product design

Most product designers do their own marker visuals for presentation to clients. They are all highly skilled draughtsmen with technical and engineering backgrounds, a fact that reveals itself in the precision of the following drawings. In fact, some of the larger design studios do employ visualizers whose job is purely to create visuals, but even their work concentrates on the technical aspect of the design.

What do product designers design?

Product designers have to be unusually versatile. For a start, they are concerned not only with the appearance of the product, but also with its function. They may work on the product at any level, from a quick restyling of an existing item to a complete design from scratch, but they will always be thinking of it as a functional object that is going to be used.

Sometimes the task begins at an even earlier stage. A design house may be asked to carry out market research to discover where there is a gap in the market which a particular product can be designed to fill. There are, of course, plenty of excellent separate market research firms which could be used instead. However, if the designer has discovered the need for a product personally, and talked to its potential buyers about what they require, he or she will have a much clearer idea of what to design.

So far, no particular product has been mentioned. This is deliberate. A good designer will be able to design anything from a corkscrew to a computer, and come up with an innovative, functional and elegant result. This is because he or she knows how people use products, and therefore is able to design items that are fit for use. Designers deliberately avoid specializing in one type of product, because such repetitive work would make them stale and reduce their creativity.

The design process

The first step is the brief: the client tells the designer what they want; or market research is done to discover exactly what is needed. When all the requirements are detailed, a budget is produced to cost the product. Often the initial brief can be met only by an impractically expensive design, in which case the specifications are scaled down to reduce the cost.

Once the designer has a clear idea of what is required, he begins to make rough sketches. Opposite is a typical page of sketches for a piece of computer hardware. The brief here was to provide a folding or retractable keyboard which can be tucked tidily out of the way when not in use, but can be brought out and used at a moment's notice. At this stage, designer David Scothron wasn't concerned with the styling of the device. In these sketches he is working out how the keyboard will retract into or against the main cabinet, and be in the right position when it is brought out for use.

From the earliest stages of the design, ergonomics is important. This is the science of people at work: how they sit at keyboards, how far they can comfortably reach, and so on. The designer asks possible users of the product to explain their jobs, and to state what they need to improve their efficiency and comfort. Sometimes a mock-up will be devised so that people can be studied as they use a machine similar to the proposed product.

The styling of a product is what everyone thinks of first when design is mentioned, and of course this is of great importance – especially in relation to selling the product. Often firms have a distinctive style with which new products have to fit in. In fact, the designer may be asked to create a house style for an entire product range, including logos, colour ranges and so on. Sometimes a firm wants a completely fresh approach, as with the radio overleaf; and that is the kind of challenge a designer really welcomes.

The designer continues to make sketches until the two or three best alternatives have been selected. Then more detailed drawings of these are made – examples are shown on the following pages – to show to the client. At the same time, if the product has mechanical or electronic parts, the designer works on the engineering aspects of the design, probably collaborating with the engineers from the client's firm.

When the client has selected the design they prefer, the engineering is worked out in detail. This includes not only the working of the device, but also how it will be manufactured – for example, designing a plastic casing so that it can be easily moulded in only two pieces which can be fitted together without complicated fastenings. Choice of materials also makes a difference to how easy a product is to manufacture, and to its cost.

The designer makes technical drawings, illustrations of the appearance of the device, and exploded views. These enable him or her, among other things, to further refine the manufacturing process. The drawings are sent to the factory, where it is worked out exactly how the product will be built.

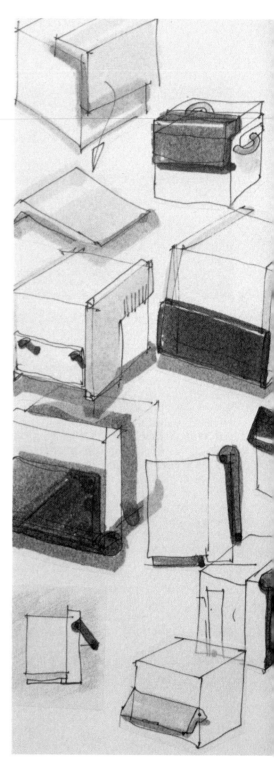

Studio: Product First/Michael Peters Group
Artist: David Scothron
Client: AVS Ltd

The sketches, below, of an auxiliary keyboard storage unit, were drawn to develop the initial concept of the product. These remained 'in house', and were not for presentation to an outside agency. The designer began by drawing each sketch on A4 typo detail paper. Edding 55 was used for the outline, and Magic Marker for the shading. He then cut out each one, and pasted them all onto a board. After this, he produced several variations deemed acceptable for presentation to the client.

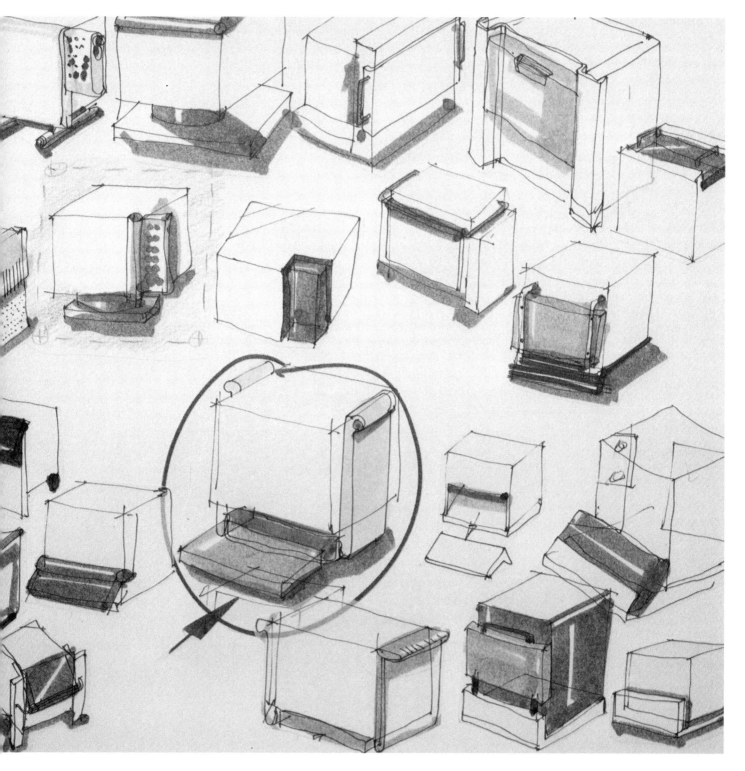

The importance of research

Common sense would seem to suggest that a portable radio should have all its controls clearly visible. However, when designer Graham Thomson and his colleagues at Product First did some research into how people actually use radios, they found that most users left their sets in one place, tuned to the same station and with the volume set to the same level. The only control they touched regularly was the on/off switch (assuming that it was not worked by the volume control knob). Therefore, the designer envisaged a radio with all the controls, except this switch, concealed. The manufacturer, Ross Electronics, wanted a radio that would look radically different from the usual near-identical, fussily styled black and silver boxes. Hiding the controls was a great help in achieving a clean appearance.

Different—but not too radical

The designer also wanted to break away from the rectangular shape of normal radios. One of his suggestions was the telescopic segmental design shown in the upper picture. The manufacturers felt that this was too eccentric, and preferred another suggestion – a smooth oblong with a hint of classical styling. The lower picture, which is the presentation visual that Graham Thomson made for the client, is almost identical to the final design as manufactured.

Can it be made?

Although the radio is assembled in Britain, the electronic parts are imported. Conventional portable radios of this size tend to have their controls positioned rather messily around the edges—an arrangement which is easy to manufacture, as the tuning condenser, volume control potentiometer and so on can be set well apart and mounted on the edge of the printed circuit, with their knobs projecting through a slot in the casing.

The designer proposed to have the controls in a neat vertical row beside a vertical tuning scale, both of these under the hinged lid which forms the left-hand part of the front of the set. The overseas electronics subcontractor protested that this couldn't be done. So Graham Thomson made a cardboard mock-up of a printed circuit with all the components arranged as he wanted. He also made a transparent model of the complete set, to show how everything fitted together. Only when he showed these to the subcontractor's engineers did they reluctantly agree that it was possible. The design agency's marketing director John Boult comments 'One of the strengths of being an outside design consultancy is that people expect you to be provocative. You're in a position of being able to question things.'

In the event, the subcontractor insisted on moving the knobs 5mm to one side, but the designer was able to accommodate this change with minimal effect on his original design.

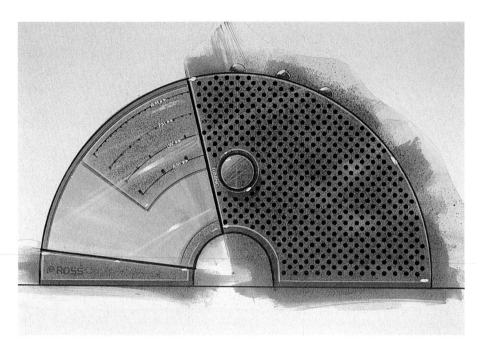

Studio: Product First/Michael Peters Group
Artist: Graham Thomson
Client: Ross Marks

Working from the client's brief for a radio with concealed controls, alternative designs (above and below) were sketched. The basic outline was drawn with fineliner, and Letraset dots represented the speaker. For the design above a diffuse tone of grey was achieved by laying a light shade on top of the paper, and a darker one on the reverse – the marker being run over the edge of the outline to create 'movement'. Details were added later, using coloured pencils and gouache.

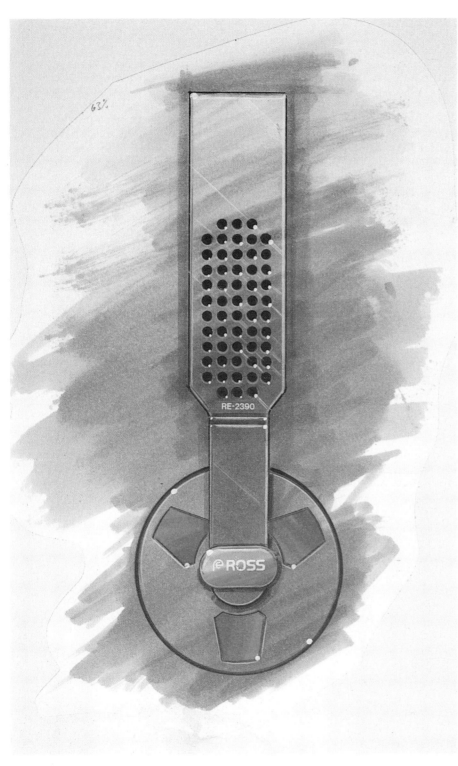

Studio: Product First/Michael Peters Group
Artist: Graham Thomson
Client: Ross Marks

The sketch, above, was one from a series for an extensive range of TV earphones. Many designs were submitted to the client, who picked those that suited his needs.

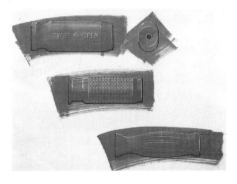

Studio: Hop
Artist: Antony Papaloizou

Initially, the designer of these firehose nozzles worked up pencil roughs, then proceeded to this simple colour illustration. Here, he laid on the background colour first, and then drew the outline on top — using crayons for shading, and gouache for highlights.

As with the other illustration of earphones from the same series (above right), once the outline was established, a darker grey was worked in on the reverse of the paper, with a lighter shade and detail applied on top. Here, though, 'cut-outs' were used for the blue to give a cleaner definition.

Designing within limitations

Antony Papaloizou's visual of a video camera, below, illustrates two points. The first is that product designers are engineers – even their marker visuals have the precision of an engineering drawing. And the second is that with many designs there is not much opportunity for innovation. Optical considerations dictated the position of the elements of the lens, its length, its diameter and the position of the control rings.

Despite this limitation, the designer has managed to create a distinctive and functional product. A typical video camera has self-consciously macho styling with aggressively projecting controls, an unnecessary amount of lettering, and so on. Antony Papaloizou has gone for a cleaner, quieter look which would also make the camera easier to use. He has also managed to bring some individuality to the design by the unusual texture of the barrel, which gives as good a grip as more conventional knurling.

Setting a style

A product designer's biggest, and often most satisfying, task is to work out a unifying style for an entire set of products. It is important to design the various items so that they are visibly all of a piece, but not of a dreary sameness. Too much unity of styling would in any case make objects less functional. It might even lead to chaos if, for example, ticket dispensers had the same styling as fire alarms. One way to unite items without imposing too much uniformity is to link them by means of a motif.

Studio: Hop
Designer/Artist: Antony Papaloizou

The illustration, below, is taken from a series drawn for the design of a video camera. This is the final visual – showing exact detail. Such work requires a very high standard of technical drawing. The outline is done in pen, and the toning is put down with Magic Marker. Pencil is used for the more detailed work. A mixture of both warm and cool greys is used to build-up the main body – Charcoal Grey for the darker shades, and Crimson, Prussian Blue and White for the details. The surface texture on the lens focus wheel is applied with black felt tip, and white gouache is used for the highlights.

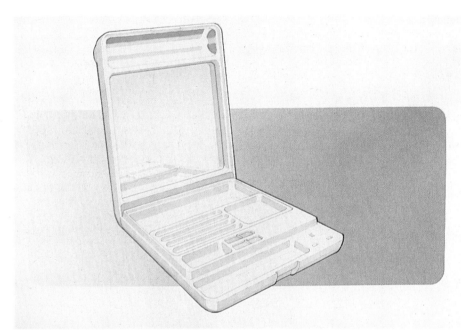

Studio: Seymour Powell
Artist: Dick Powell
Client: Clairol

It is always difficult to render white objects – you need the very minimum of marks so that the white of the paper does most of the work, as in the visual left.

Studio: Seymour Powell
Artist: Mike Armstrong
Client: Philips

This rendered elevational view shows shape, proportion, detail and construction. Marker has been freely combined with pastel, crayon and other media to create a fast, informative impression that is just as much a working drawing as a finished presentation visual.

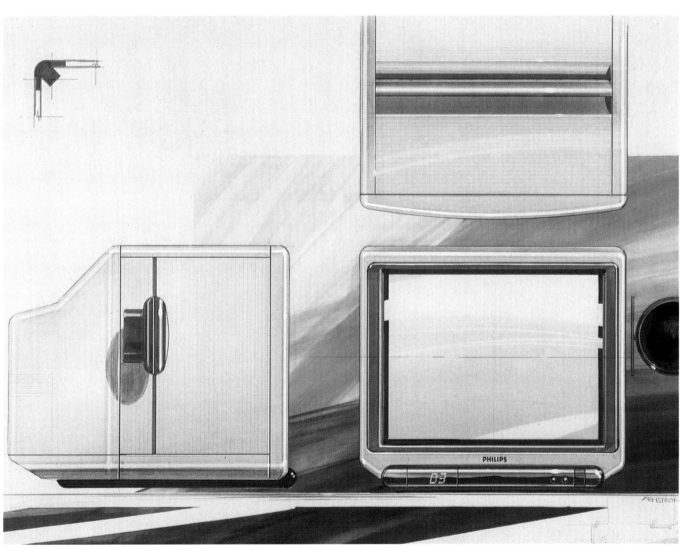

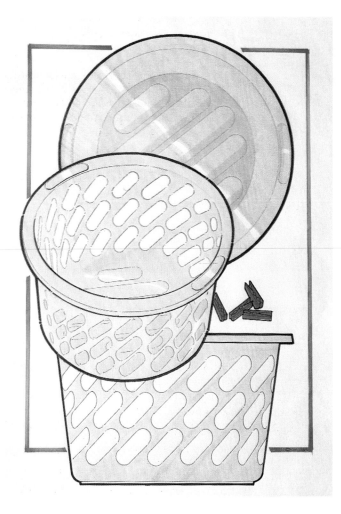

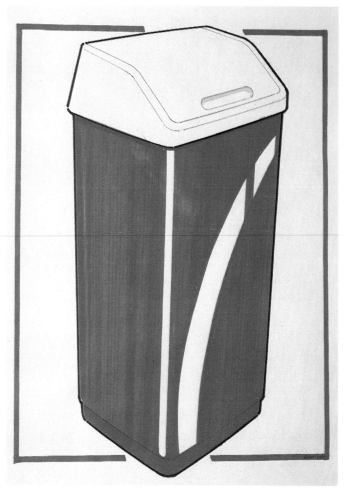

Tickling the client's fancy

Engineering precision in drawings is one thing, making them appeal to the client is another. It is difficult to make a plastic washing-up bowl or a kitchen rubbish bin attractive. In this case the bowl had already been designed, and the visual was simply to present the new season's colour.

The shape of a swingbin can't be changed much, as the bin part is formed in a simple two-piece mould, and therefore has to be smooth and slightly tapering towards the bottom. However, the design of the swinging top has been improved by tilting it towards the user, which would avoid the irritating tendency of symmetrical swingbin flaps to swing out and fall back, knocking the rubbish out of your hand onto the floor.

To make the visuals attractive and persuasive to the store buyers, artist Chris Garcin has adopted a simplified, light style and has used a decorative border. These drawings are parts of a series that was presented to the buyers, showing different suggestions for, colourways. The products themselves form part of ranges of kitchen equipment which are constantly being added to and reissued in new colours. Every change requires a new set of presentation visuals.

Studio: Wharmby Associates
Artist: Chris Garcin
Client: Mendle Brothers Ltd

Both of the illustrations, above, show products sold through Habitat and John Lewis. The range has been regularly updated and added to for the past 5 years. These visuals are used by the suppliers for presentation to the store buyers. Because some products in the range are up to 3ft high, the illustrations have to be fairly representational, otherwise the client may have difficulty visualizing the actual item. Here, Letraset marker paper and Pantone markers were used. The outlines were drawn in black permanent ink pen. Super Warm Red was used for the main body of the swingbin and for both borders, and Pantone 115 (beige) was used for colouring the bowls.

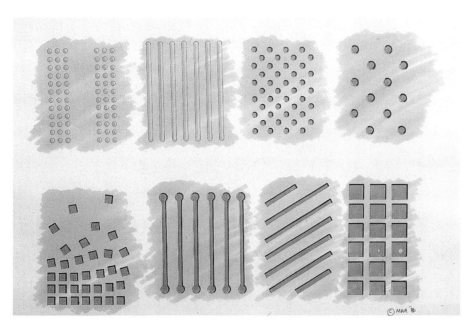

Studio: Wharmby Associates
Artist: Andrew Davey
Client: Esselte Dymo

An illustration, left, of a design for a lettertray. A light blue was laid down first, on Letraset. Details were added with a Pantone dark marker. Highlights were picked out in pencil.

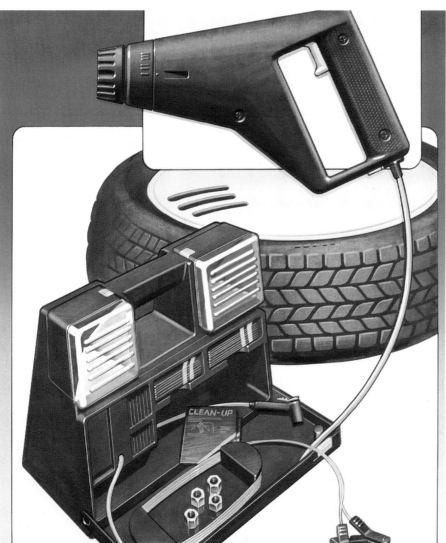

Studio: Seymour Powell

Matt black can be rendered quickly and easily using Black, Cool Greys and white crayon and pastel. Here, each element was produced separately, and then they were all assembled on the air-brushed background.

Automotive rendering

Marker renders the glossy paintwork of a car as no other drawing medium can, thanks to its intense, brilliant colours. At the same time it causes technical problems. A visual has to convey an accurate impression of the shape of the vehicle, and for this it is necessary to gradate or fade the colours. To achieve this, marker is combined with other media, of which the most useful is pastel mixed with talcum powder.

Design from the inside out

The bodywork of a car is only the clothing of its mechanical parts and its passenger and baggage space. Even the most speculative and futuristic designs have to be based on a clear idea of how these parts will be arranged. And those designs that are not mere dreams also have to take into account the manufacturing processes for forming body panels and glass, as well as legal regulations covering such matters as the height of fittings like bumpers and headlamps.

Car stylists, even those employed by firms that produce the most ordinary vehicles, spend a lot of time designing 'dream cars' that are most unlikely to be built. Most of the visuals on the following pages are by students from the Royal College of Art in London, but the principle is the same. Only by indulging in a great deal of speculation is the artist likely to come up with a new, attractive and useful idea which can be taken up and put into production.

Who designs cars?

Designers of cars or other vehicles may be employed in the design studio of an automobile manufacturer, or they may work in a firm which creates exterior or interior designs for manufacturers' projected new models. An example of such a firm is Italdesign in Italy, which has designed, among many other successful cars, the original Volkswagen Golf, the Fiat Panda and the Lotus Esprit.

There is an intermediate kind of firm, the coachbuilder, which designs special bodies or adaptations of existing cars, and may also create designs for mass-produced models. For example, the Italian firm of Pininfarina not only designed the Peugeot 205 for Peugeot itself to build, but has also designed, and now manufactures, a convertible version of the same car. Coachbuilders often design and build 'one-off' prototypes which are exhibited at motor shows. Many, though by no means all, of these are just styling exercises and are not driveable cars. Sometimes one-off designs are later transformed into actual production cars. A curious example is the Alfa Romeo Duetto two-seater sports car. The body was designed by Pininfarina in the mid-1950s and exhibited at the Turin show. Nearly twenty years later Alfa Romeo began to produce a car with this body design almost unaltered—though a good deal of restyling work has been done on it since.

Volume car manufacturers also build and exhibit one-off prototypes, which they like to call 'concept cars', as the design is intended to embody an idea of future car design. A recent example is Ford's Eltec, so named because it makes every conceivable use of electronic technology. Often concept cars later go into production in a modified form. Examples are Austin Rover's Princess models, which went into production in 1980; and, more recently, the current Ford Sierra. Manufacturers see concept cars as a useful way of doing market research by exposing their ideas to motoring correspondents and the public.

Artist: Michael Ani

For this visual the artist used pencil outline, Cadmium Red marker, pastel with talcum powder, and Derwent pencil lines.

A 'dream bike'

Alex Padwa, the designer whose project is illustrated on the following four pages, has taken the idea of the motorcycle and sidecar and drastically reworked it. This is a 'dream bike', but it is also a perfectly feasible project. It could be built tomorrow with existing motorcycle parts hung on a suitable frame—though some modifications would have to be made to improve the view from the cockpit, to give some ground clearance at the bottom of the wheel fairings and to sort out the little matter of steering the front wheel.

The conventional arrangement of motorcycle and sidecar has some advantages: cheapness; simplicity; a reasonable carrying capacity of three people and a little baggage; and, in most countries, a low rate of taxation compared with a car. Its main disadvantages are instability caused by uneven weight distribution, and lack of weather protection, at least for the people on the motorcycle half of the combination.

Alex Padwa has overcome these disadvantages by moving the riders into an enclosed cockpit in the middle (though there is only room for two). This arrangement is lower and considerably better aerodynamically. The design is also a bravura exercise in thoroughly unusual shapes.

Designer: Alex Padwa

1. The designer develops shape and perspective with ballpoint on layout paper.

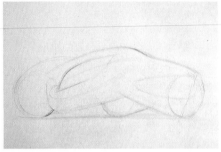

2. A soft Derwent pencil allows the designer to produce lines of any required thickness, giving a preliminary idea of the distribution of shading and weight in the final work.

3. A further development of the ideas worked out in stage 2. This is a separate drawing and not a reworking of the previous one, although it is done in the same medium of Derwent pencil.

4. The designer uses a Cadmium Red Magic Marker for the areas of red paintwork, leaving white paper to indicate reflections. Applying several layers of colour deepens the tone to some extent.

5. A dark grey marker is used to give depth to the vehicle's cockpit canopy, and to indicate the shadow it casts on the ground. Skill is needed to maintain the smooth outline of the red and grey oval.

6. Scraping some pastel onto a sample of paper to test its effect, which varies with the paper. Pastel is used to give fine gradations of colour for shading and reflections, which indicate form.

8. The designer first uses grey pastel mixed with talcum to accentuate the shadows, then pastel of the same red as the marker, also mixed with talcum, to add the softer reflections to the body.

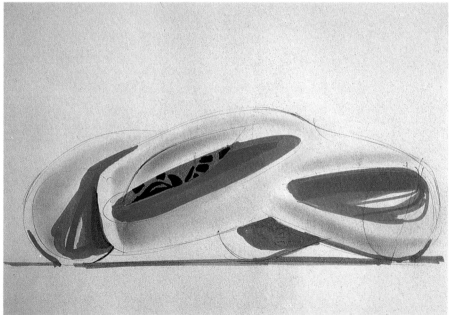

7. Talcum powder is mixed with the pastel to give a smooth application and finish when applied to the marker. Talcum may also be used alone to soften colour. Both are applied with a piece of cotton wool.

9. A little yellow pastel is used for soft, light-coloured reflections in the red areas. The designer has added detail in dark grey marker to indicate the interior seen through the canopy.

10. The designer adds black Derwent pencil lines to accentuate the form of the canopy, and to show the reflection, in the underside of the wheel fairing, of the dark shadow the vehicle casts on the ground.

12. The designer uses a red Derwent pencil to give greater depth to the red, and reduce its brightness. This also gives a better gradation from the red marker into the two shades of pastel which run up to it.

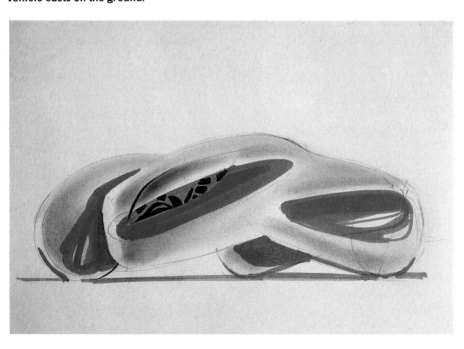

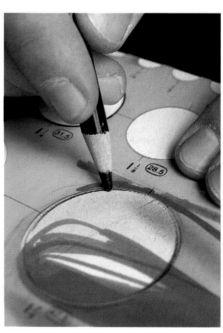

11. More grey pastel is added over the red on the inside of the far wheel fairing to give extra shading, and also to other areas of the body to increase the impression of solidity.

13. A circle stencil is used to draw the outline of the removable wheel-cover panel, which also adds to the three-dimensional effect of the body. White pencil will be used to highlight the edges.

14. More grey marker on the underside, and further touches of red, strengthen the modelling. Note the solidity that the black and white pencil lines give to the 'shut lines' of the wheel cover.

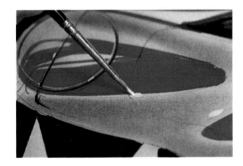

15. The designer adds a few highlights in white gouache to increase the effect of glossy paintwork. These brilliant white touches also help to make the picture stand out from the paper.

16. Top right: Black Derwent pencil is used for the 'shut lines' of the canopy, the edge of its transparent Perspex, and the wheel cover on the front fairing. This further defines the form of the body.
Right: Alex Padwa working on this drawing. Note the sheet of paper which he uses as a palette for trying out different colour combinations. This must be of the same paper as the drawing itself.

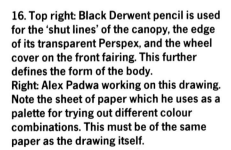

Off the road

The next four pages show the development of one visual of a four-wheel-drive cross-country vehicle that is nevertheless comfortable and stylish – a successor to the Range Rover. This is considerably more than a styling exercise, as designer Anthony Lo has worked out the mechanical arrangements in some detail in other drawings. He also made visuals of the car from other viewpoints, and continued from this stage to make a clay scale model. The design is his final project at the Royal College of Art, and is unlikely to be continued beyond this model. Nevertheless, a working vehicle could certainly be built on the basis of the design, though one might criticize the lack of protection for the meticulously drawn headlamps, and wonder about the practicality of the ultra-low-profile tyres on a very rough surface.

Clay models are used as a stage in the design of production cars, and making them is a necessary skill for the designer. The first model is quite small, typically 50cm long, and is a useful means of verifying the appearance of the design from all angles. After a design has been approved, a full-size clay model is constructed. This is shaped with great accuracy, since it is used to take measurements for making the press tools with which the steelwork of the car body is stamped. In the case of a car with GRP or Kevlar bodywork, it is used directly to make the female moulds in which the body parts will be formed.

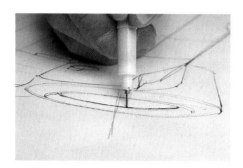

Designer: Anthony Lo

1. The designer plans his drawing of an off-road vehicle with a sketch on A3 paper.

2. Once he has the dimensions and perspective right, he enlarges the sketch on to A2, and again checks the perspective and ellipses. He likes to draw straight lines freehand, without using a ruler.

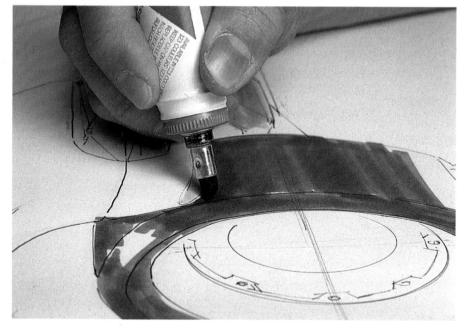

3. He uses a C7 Cool Grey Magic Marker to indicate the shape of the tyre. Several different tones of grey can be achieved with one marker by repeated application.

4. A darker grey is used for the wheel arch and other dark areas, and a lighter one, C4, for the shadows and reflections on the body and to outline the rear tyre – here, the faintness gives an idea of distance.

5. Detail of the previous picture, showing how several shades of Cool Grey are used to model the tyre, suspension strut and air intake, and to give the darker tones of the complex reflection in the headlamp.

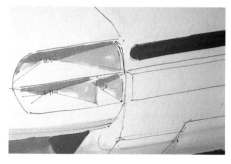

6. Detail of the other headlamp unit. Two tones of Cool Grey indicate the parabolic reflectors of the three parts of the lamp, but considerably more work will be needed to give a realistic impression.

7. Three shades of Cool Grey are used for the tyre and the shadow of the wheel arch, and white paper is left to form the highlight on the tyre. This shows how the paper itself can be used as a colour.

8. The designer scrapes off some pastel onto paper of the same type as used for the drawing. He will mix the three colours to get the shade for the glass and engine cover, adding talcum powder for smoothness.

9. Top: Pastels and talcum are blended with cotton wool to give various shades.

10. Above: The mixture is applied, working outwards to fade it to almost nothing.

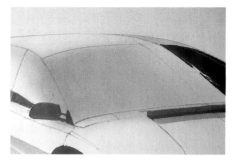

11. The shading of the windscreen and side windows gives a strong impression of the curve of the glass. The dramatic black reflection on the right is read as that of a building behind the car.

12. Pastel can also be applied directly with the stick. Here, a white stick is being used to add a bright highlight to one of the headlamp reflectors. The effect is not as strong as that of white gouache.

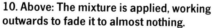

13. The whole car, showing how pastel adds to the form, softens the line and increases the lustre of the body. Not all the shadow has been added yet.

14. The designer mixes yellow and black pastel for the shadows and reflections on the front underside of the car. The warmer tone, reflecting the ground, contrasts with the bluish sky tones in the glass.

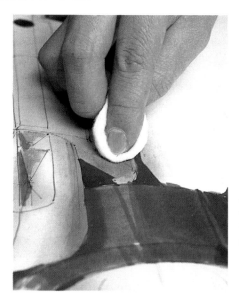

15. He adds the pastel only to those areas which pick up reflections from the ground. If this shade were added to any other areas, the effect would be lost.

16. The whole drawing, after the warm shading has been added. Compare it with stage 13 to see how the modelling has been strengthened. A touch of orange has also been added for the indicator lens.

17. A streak of dark grey charcoal pencil deepens the body side moulding behind the wheel arch. The dark area is a reflection of the imaginary dark ground under the car, rather than an actual shadow.

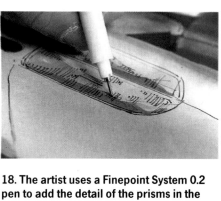

18. The artist uses a Finepoint System 0.2 pen to add the detail of the prisms in the lens of the light unit. These disposable pens almost give the finish of a Rapidograph, and do not get clogged.

19. He strengthens the contours of the body by darkening the lines with a fine Pentel and a curve – even he finds it difficult to retrace a curve freehand without getting a double line.

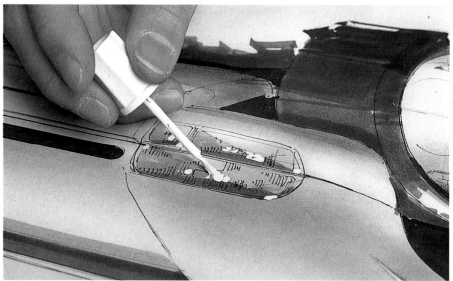

20. To finish the headlights, he adds highlights with white Tipp-Ex correction fluid, which he says works just as well as gouache. (But if it is used over coloured marker, the colour stains the white.)

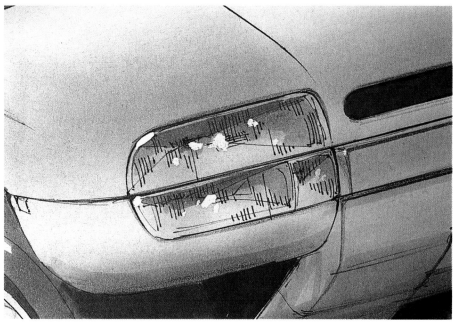

21. Above: A streak of white pastel is added, working directly with the stick, to highlight the moulding on the side panel above the wheel, an effect further enhanced by the thin black line above.

22. Below: To 'fix' the car in position on the paper, the artist has added some C7 Cool Grey marker to give a hint of the ground, though the full shadow which the car would cast is not shown.

23. Above: Anthony Lo at work. In front of him is a side view of the same vehicle, and underneath it a drawing of the mechanical layout – showing that it is a serious project and no mere stylist's fantasy.

Anthony Lo's other degree project: a design for a time trial bicycle with an aerodynamic carbon fibre frame and disc wheels.

Top left: A finished visual, mainly in Magic Marker Cool Greys, layered to achieve the shading on the lower half of the wheel. The paper is left white for the lettering and the highlights on the frame. Shadows are added in pastel, and the outlines are strengthened with dark Derwent pencil.

Bottom left: A measured sketch, done with a Finepoint System pen on grid paper to determine the dimensions, and including an outline of the rider. He worked out the basic idea in several preliminary sketches.

Top right: The other side of the bicycle in a different colour scheme, executed in three Cool Greys and Black Magic Marker. The bottom tube supporting the rear wheel is different, since on the right side the tube encloses part of the chain.

Bottom right: The left side in a version of the first scheme but with a red frame.

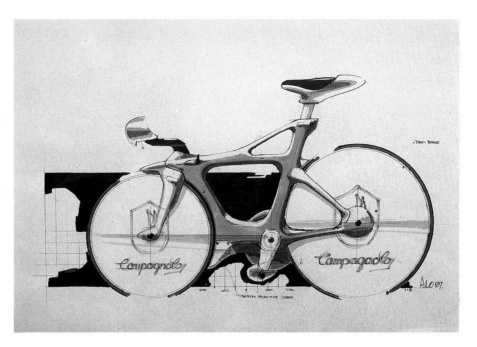

Interiors

It is unusual for the same person to design both the exterior and the interior of a car. Manufacturers feel that the skills involved are different. However, Lotus Design prefer their designers to do both in the interests of achieving a well-integrated overall design. The adjoining picture is a visual by Lotus designer Simon Cox for the interior of the low-cost two-seater Lotus sports car, due for launch in 1989. The interiors on the opposite page are by Royal College of Art students, and are 'dream' projects rather than designs intended for manufacture.

The exploded view

Mathias Kulla's off-road vehicle is more utilitarian than Anthony Lo's, but just as thoroughly designed. An exploded view is a highly useful way of showing a mechanical layout, especially for presentation to a client who can't read a standard engineering drawing. It is also often helpful in working out how a product will be manufactured. The GRP parts—the body and the boatlike, watertight interior shell— would actually be manufactured and fitted together over the frame in much the same way as shown in this illustration.

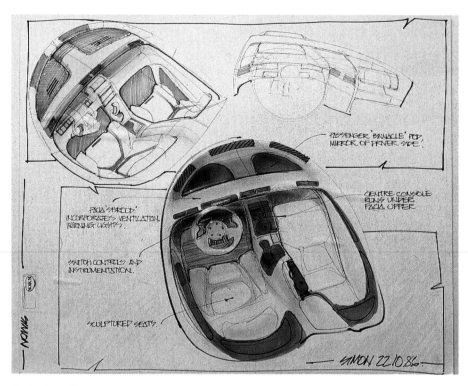

Studio: Lotus Design
Artist: Simon Cox

For this interior design for a sports car, the artist used Biensang Fine Art Newsprint, a textured non-bleedproof paper, because he likes the way it makes the colours bleed. Preliminary sketches were done in ballpoint, and marker colours were laid down on the final ballpoint sketch, using both sides of the paper for the darker shades to achieve greater intensity on this absorbent surface. The shadows and textures are worked in grey pastel with talcum powder. The yellow background is in Prisma crayon followed by pastel.

Artist: Mathias Kulla

A project to develop a successor to the Land Rover, with greater interior space but smaller exterior dimensions. The mid-engined design uses a Lotus backbone chassis with greatly raised suspension, shown in the exploded view right, and a GRP body. Designers usually have to fit their work over a predetermined mechanical layout. The original A3 sketch was redrawn on A2 and filled in with marker, using layers and nib strokes to achieve reflections.

Artist: Mathias Kulla

Above: An interior for a car similar to a Ford Fiesta, though the original idea was for a smaller model. The designer feels that small car designs should not be too soft. Marker colours are laid down on his second A3 ballpoint sketch, using both sides, and pastel highlights and reflections and dark Derwent pencil outlines added.

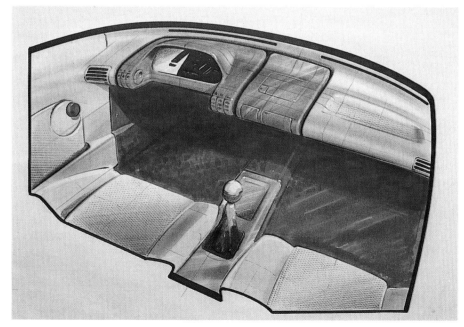

Artist: Michael Ani

Left: In this interior the designer's idea is to incorporate all the features into a single form. He uses a tracing of his original outline drawing for a highly finished visual, or the drawing itself for a rough one. As well as the usual techniques, he uses a Derwent pencil with a rubber mat under the paper to give texture.

Miscellaneous projects

The design of commercial vehicles is as important as that of cars, and in some ways more demanding. A truck driver spends his entire working day in his cab, so its interior design really matters.

Designer: Alex Padwa

This minibus is highly aerodynamic, and thus both economical and stable. The raked floor allows all passengers to see out of the front. The drawing, on marker paper, uses layers of very light Warm and Cool Greys, with a pastel background and Derwent lines.

Artist: Douglas Barber

Working on both sides of heavy-grade draughting film to achieve three-dimensional depth, the artist blocked in the colours with black, red and cool grey markers. The blue bodywork was built up with pastel on cotton pads.

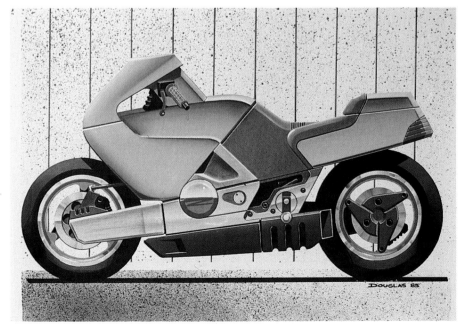

Artist: Mathias Kulla

An entry for a German magazine competition (right) to find the successor to the Volkswagen Golf. It was meant to look appropriate 20 years from now, but still to refer to the soft lines of the old VW Beetle. The pencil design was worked up to A2 size on American Vellum paper. Ink stays wet for some time on this paper, making colour blending easy. The deep shadows were achieved by using dark grey marker on both sides of the paper. He also used marker on the back of the paper with pastel on the front, giving a very even finish with an attractive texture (caused by the grain of the paper).

Artist: Douglas Barber

This drawing was cut out and fixed to a separate background. The artist used ballpoint for the outline because it gives a freer look, though sometimes he uses a fine fibre-tip pen instead. He begins colouring with the darker shadows and tones, and works through to the lightest shades. If he wants extra depth of colour in the light areas he applies the same colour again, accentuating the three-dimensional effect. He uses dark grey and black Derwent pencils to sharpen outlines, though the outermost outline is bound to be sharp because of the cutting-out process. Once the drawing has been fitted into its background he adds shadows and highlights.

Studio: Lotus Design
Designer: Julian Thompson

This external design for a sports car for Lotus began with rough sketches in ballpoint. He lays the final one under a sheet of Vellum paper and roughly traces the outline in ballpoint. When adding colours he uses the back of the paper for darker shades, which allows him to build up intensity and depth of colour to render the reflective quality of metal. He uses pastel and talcum powder to soften the contours and forms of the body. The interior details are in black marker on the back of the paper, with the blue reflections over them on the front, which adds to the three-dimensional effect. The red pastel shades are deepened with blue and purple pastel. Highlights and lettering are in white gouache and the background Flo-master ink through an airbrush.

9 Architectural, interior and exhibition design

Marker has taken a long time to reach acceptance in this area of design, and is still avoided by some practitioners. The advent of the marker in the sixties was received with some degree of caution by environmental and exhibition designers. As their world is one of habitable space that is depicted at small scale, they considered the early felt-tips to be too crude. Instead, they relegated them to the role of visualizing and evolving new ideas and the colour-coding of generative diagrams.

There were other reasons for the initial lack of response to this new medium. The late fifties was a period still in the grip of International Modernism and, set against its associated starkness and austerity, colour seemed to appear as an afterthought and, consequently, was denied any major role in the design process. Architectural, interior and exhibition design tended to derive from the clutch pencil and the technical pen, whose delineations might occasionally be tinted for public consumption. The concept of the creation of built space, and the objects that it might contain, as a colourless science was underpinned by a lack of colour teaching in design schools and a corresponding lack of colour illustration in the design magazines of the day. By contrast, a resurgence of interest in colour in the sixties

coincided with the more widespread use of polychrome reproduction, which revealed a new generation of designers who were already experimenting with colour on and in their buildings. Indeed, when Le Corbusier's work from the thirties and forties became republished in colour, his brightly painted architecture came as something of a shock to those who had, hitherto, misconceived of his buildings as colourless essays in raw concrete.

Furthermore, environmental designers had been traditionally schooled in the application of flat, immaculate transparent washes using mediums such as watercolour and Chinese and India ink. The fact that the early marker could not achieve sufficient precision meant that its debut in presentation graphics had to await the ensuing

advances in marker technology. Meanwhile, it became confined to specific roles. Markers were worked on the underside of translucent sheets or rendered on to underlays over which transparent line drawings were hung. In both cases, this indirect technique was employed to provide a muted colour impression for the client-viewer.

Markers were also to find an unusual role in dyeline printing – a process central to environmental design, and one demanding that originals are produced on transparent materials. Here, markers were introduced to tracing paper production drawings to produce a range of washes and stipples which, when printed, reproduced as a sophisticated scale of textured greys. However, it was the developing need to colour dyeline prints that led to the marker being firmly established in the

environmental design process. It was found that, unlike the dimensional distortion caused by watercolour, markers could be worked directly on to dyeline print papers. And they could simulate rapidly a wide range of spatial effects at different drawing scales. Also, dyeline papers provided an excellent and inexpensive surface on which marker inks automatically became muted – a visual quality particularly important when depicting space. Furthermore, if a drawing was ruined when working against the pressure of deadlines, designers could simply use another print without having to redraft the outline from scratch.

The acceptance of markers in the design studios of the seventies coincided with a new development in architecture and interior design – the 'high-tech' style – which, towards the end of the decade, began to turn the paraphernalia of industry into an art form. The arrival of high-tech also heralded the deployment of a brilliant and synthetic colour in architectural space. This was a trend that unleashed the marker – not as a vehicle for colouring diagrams, but as a positive means of diagramming the colour-coded components of an industrial style. Possibly the brightly coloured claddings of this period owe more to the magic of markers than to any other medium!

Meanwhile, interior and exhibition designers had become aware of, and influenced by, a highly professional-looking marker technique that had emerged from the disciplines of automative, industrial, and product design. These stylish, controlled but apparently spontaneous images of prototypes – often executed at full scale – had expanded the marker vocabulary. This technique was adopted quickly because the speed at which markers could simulate the 'difficult' finishes, such as wood, tile, and fabric, and produce convincing representations of reflective surfaces, such as glass, chrome, and water, meant that the marker had finally come of age.

Architects, too, had begun to experiment with techniques that could cope with buildings that were now designed with a greater sense of colour and decoration. They discovered that markers could replicate the scaled appearance of a vast range of building materials, light conditions, and atmospherics. Their elevations were now turned out using markers because, via the application of horizontal bands of appropriately coloured inks, the hitherto painstaking process of showing masonry could now be accomplished at great speed. Also, the rendition of glazing (an habitual problem for the architect) was overcome using the more subtle blues and greys.

Studio: PA Design/Michael Peters Group
Artist: Chris Murray

The illustrations of bathroom fittings (below) were produced so a client could visualize his product 'in situ'. Initially, he chose from several alternatives pasted up on a board. From these, rough sketches were drawn and then traced off, to scale, on to marker layout paper. The outline was drawn in with rollerball felt tip. Flat colour was laid on with Magic Marker, and crayon was used for shadow and highlighting the edges. Throughout there was constant contact between the designer and the engineers working for the manufacturer.

Artist: Claire Norbury

These illustrations are sections of the plans for a Ladies Spa and Health Club. The work involved the redesign and rebuilding of Victorian swimming baths. Both designs were drawn with a hard pencil, directly onto mounting board. The outlines were scored with a scalpel, to stop the marker colours bleeding over them. Right: Brick White was used for the pale shades and Warm Grey for tone and shadow. Darker shades were built up with Pale Blue and Pantone 351, and the palm trees were outlined with a black Rotring pen. Below: Pale Blue marker was used for the patio, built up in layers to deepen the tone. Density and texture were added to the shaded areas, with crayon. A wash of Cool Shadow, followed by Light Green, was laid down for the water, and white crayon was used for highlights. Shadows and tones in the stonework were put in with Brick White.

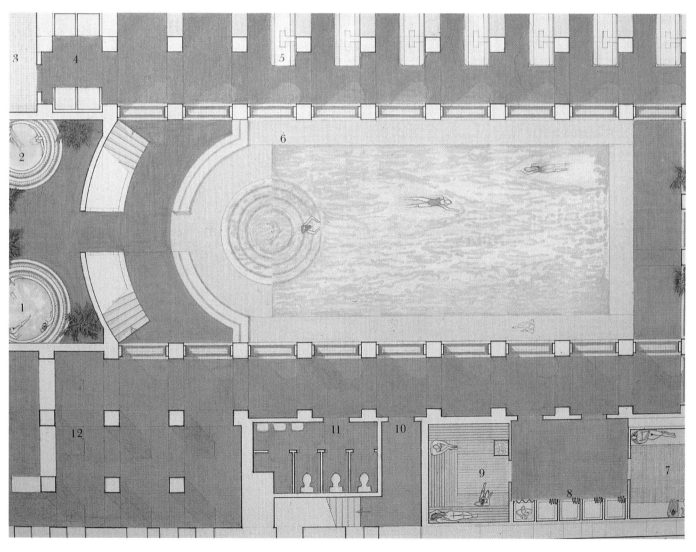

Artist: Miranda Ottewill

Right: this is taken from a series of collage type roughs drawn for a project to develop a hospice. The designer researched the idea by visiting various hospices and investigating their particular needs through talking to staff. Initially, her ideas were developed by drawing on blackboard, utilizing bold shapes and colours, at this stage, as a design aid. The highly finished visuals produced for presentation were worked directly onto marker layout paper, without first drawing pencil roughs. Magic Markers were used for the large areas of colour and Pentel pen for the detail.

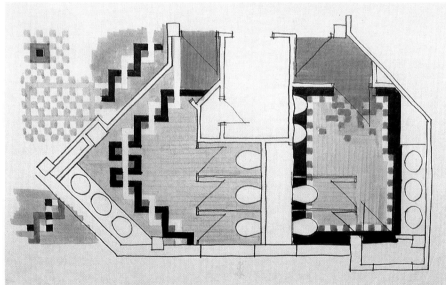

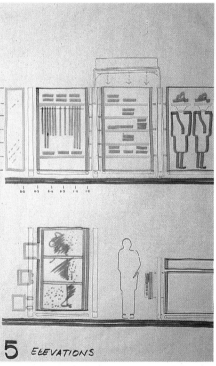

Studio: Brennan Whalley Ltd
Artist: Dennis Brennan

A floor plan of new offices. The corporate identity was developed from the client's brief for a very brash, noticeable colour scheme, and their colours are used in this design. The artist worked on non-bleed detail paper, and used black, Pentel fine-tips pens for the outline, Magic Markers for colouring, and the paper itself as white.

Studio: Jiricna Kerr
Artist: Kathy Kerr

A first sketch, presentation-level visual, from a series of 20 of an 'in-store' storage system for the fashion house, Planet. Initially, a pencil rough was drawn up, followed by freehand overlays with Pentel fine pens. Colour was added using a combination of Magic Marker and fluorescent Stabilo markers.

Studio: Brennan Whalley Ltd
Artist: Martin Roche

The visuals shown here and on the opposite page are taken from a series intended to illustrate various activities available in a Children's Experience Centre, proposed for the Liverpool area. Drawing on research into similar centres in the United States, the agency carried out a feasibility study before presenting alternative ideas to the client. Non-bleed detail paper was used throughout. The outlines of the plans were drawn with black Pentel fine-tip pens. Colour was laid down with Magic Markers— the agency likes them because their free-flowing quality allows the designer a greater freedom of colour and movement than is possible with other media. Where white is required the paper is utilised. For final presentations to a client they sometimes produce visuals airbrushed in Magic Marker ink.

Right: a wind tunnel that would allow children to walk through it and experience windforce. It would include a model to demonstrate how the wind affects a plane taking-off.

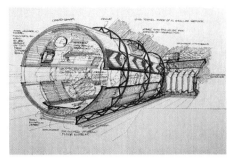

Right and below: a remote-controlled robot arm that would allow children to coordinate its movements through a computer.

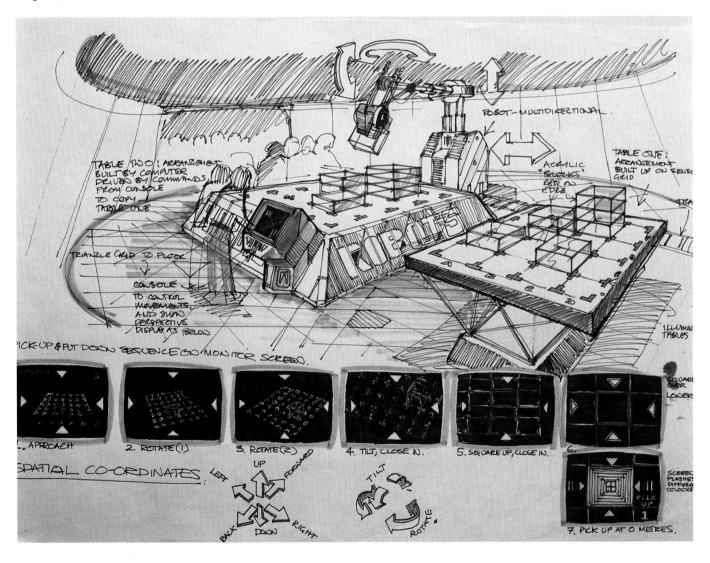

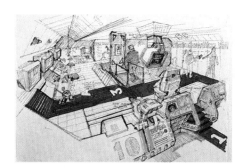

Left and below: computers linked to exercise bicycles that would enable children to measure their heart rates, and teach them how to cope with their various physical abilities.

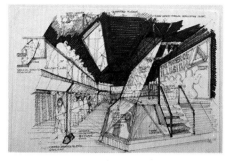

Above: a raised area that would work as a theatre, where children could dress-up and act out a play.

The contemporary use of marker

By the eighties some distinctive techniques had evolved which combined markers with other mediums, such as airbrush, crayons and, particularly, coloured pencils. However, a typical marker perspective begins with a line drawing in pencil, technical pen, or razor point marker. Areas of colour are next established employing a co-ordinated scale of colour strength to fix foreground, middleground, and background, and using graded washes to indicate varying degrees of illumination on larger surfaces. To complete the illusion of three-dimensional modelling, shades and shadows are finally intensified with darker markers. There are several variations of this technique, one of the most common being the colour modification of marker washes and the insertion of highlights using a range of light-coloured pencils.

This technique can range from appearing visually fast and loose, as in a sketch, to being worked up into a highly polished drawing. Apart from its obvious use in perspectives and elevations, the

Studio: Leslie Millard Associates
Artist: Les Causton

Left, above and opposite: four stand designs from the 'Food for Britain' Exhibition. Pencil sketches were developed from the original plans by overlay tracing. At each stage of the trace-off more detail was added until the pencil outline drawing was considered satisfactory. The outline was traced off in black ink, Magic Marker was used for the main blocks of colour and the highlights were worked in with pastel and gouache. Blue pastel was used for the reflections in the glass cabinets, and a cut-out mask was applied so that the background could be sprayed-in with aerosol paint.

Left: a visual for a shopping centre in Wimbledon. Having established a satisfactory angle of elevation, the outline was filled in with Magic Markers—applied in layers to build up the darker tones. The shadows were formed by masking off these areas and applying aerosol paint spray. Finally, the entire visual was sprayed with white paint to diffuse the sharpness of the image.

same technique is also applied to sections and plans in order to provide clarity, luminosity, and an all-important sense of space. Although generally applied to white drawing surfaces, some designers believe that the marker technique is enhanced when rendered on toned papers, such as medium-toned blue- and brown-line dyeline print papers and yellow tracing paper.

In the face of such a vast spectrum of marker ink colours, trial palettes of colour are invariably tested on a scrap of the same drawing paper to be used in the final artwork. This is done to evaluate the effect of individual colours in the selected scheme, but also to test their combined impression when superimposed as washes. This prelude to artwork is a symptom of a greater awareness of colour and its dimensions of hue, chroma (saturation, or colour strength), and value (lightness) in design. For instance, designers find that the more limited palettes, that is, those restricted to a number of shades of one colour have the greatest presentation impact. Even more important with markers is to make a trial assessment of chromatic strength, because this is the colour dimension that promotes the illusion of space and depth. Therefore, each main colour within a palette should be supported by several markers whose inks will provide a progressive weakening (desaturation) of the main colour as it moves back into the space of the drawing. Another crucial factor that must be determined before work commences is the tonal scale of values because it is the light and dark relationships of the finished artwork that will ultimately project its essential structure.

Having tamed the marker, architects, interior and exhibition designers have found a modern successor to the more time-consuming watercolour technique. Together with coloured pencils, markers are now by far the most prevalent colour-drawing medium in design studios and offices. Being inextricably linked to the revival in the orchestration of environmental colour, it seems possible that the felt-tipped marker has been responsible for our modern experience of a more colourful and more variegated man-made environment.

Studio: Design House Studio
Artist: Nigel Langford

The designer used this visual of a Muswell's Cafe Bar, above, both as a rough, whilst developing the design, and for presentation to the client. Having used pencil to establish the interior layout of the cafe, a waterbased fineliner was used for the outline — this will not bleed when marker colours are applied. He worked from light to dark, building up the colours in layers, and utilizing the white of the paper, rather than applying gouache. The highlights were worked out to a 90 degree angle, using a set-square. This gives a neater appearance.

Left: one of a series of visuals produced for a chain of American-style diners. The clients were the New England Restaurant Group, so the artist chose an appropriate style, using American country inns as a reference. The techniques employed were the same as for his illustrations opposite and below. Note the absence of figures in these visuals. The artist feels that their inclusion would distract the client's attention away from the design.

The brief for the illustration below was to convert Williamson's Library Bar, in London, into a gentlemen's smoking room. The designer used part of the Albert Hall as a reference to design the Etruscan-style floor tiles. Again, the colours were built up in layers, working from light to dark. The rich colour used on the walls was Oxblood.

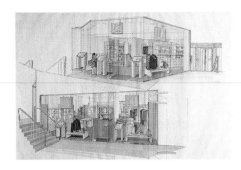

Artist: Brian Alldridge
Client: Alfred Dunhill

**Three visuals taken from a series produced
for Dunhill. The designer and the artist
worked together to develop the style of the
storage fixtures. Initially, a very detailed
sketch was worked up in stages, tracing
from detailed drawings of individual units
onto marker paper. The artist was trying to
obtain a crispness of line and colour so he
chose Entwhistle and Thorpe marker paper,
which does not allow colour to spread too
far. This was specially important where two
shades were used side by side. Coloured
details were put in with Pentel water-based
pens. Pantone was used for the paler
shades. The glass highlights were produced
in tones of grey — colours which pick-up and
simulate reflections, and a fine line of crisp
colour was added by the application of a
little paint to the edge of the counters.
In the large visual (right) the artist used
Barely Beige for the background, and a light**

Suntan for the wood finish of the shelving.
Where darker shades were required they
were built up in layers, using Mahogany or
Dark Suntan — although the artist finds that
the paper can absorb only 3 or 4 layers of
colour before they become unstable.

Note, when details are put in with Pentel
water-based pens before marker colour is
applied, then some of their 'crispness' will
be lost. So, the sequence in which Pentel
pen and marker is used will depend upon
the desired effect.

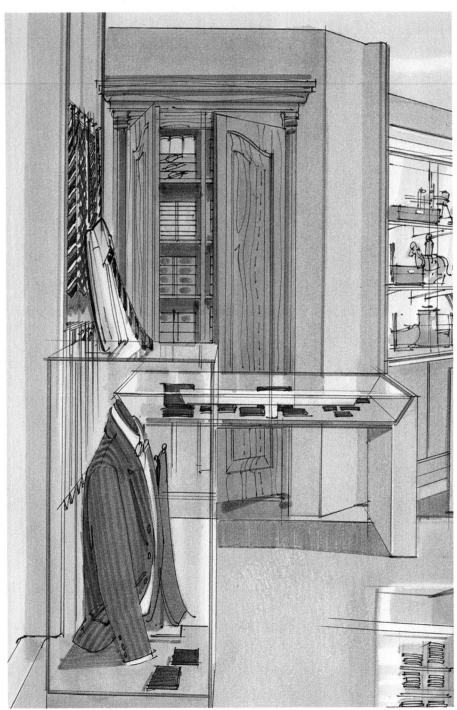

Artist: Brian Alldridge
Client: Alfred Dunhill

Below: an earlier scheme for the designs opposite. The finished visual was cut out and mounted on a studland-type grey board to give it a sense of distance. Because this type of visual is planned to fit the client's marketing concept, often the drawing is used as a guide by the developer, and is referred to just as much as the plan is.

Artist: Terry Lewis

Below: a concept drawing for the redevelopment of the Royal Corn Exchange in Bradford, as a shopping precinct. The artist referred to architect's drawings of the existing building, and thumbnail sketches of the proposed changes. Also, he was provided with picture references relating to colour, type of stonework etc. After working out a pencil rough, to establish perspective, on Letraset Marker paper, he traced off the outline onto a new sheet of A2 paper, using black fineliner. He put the colour in with Brick White and beiges, warm greys 1–7 for the iron structural work, and white gouache for highlights on the glass shopfronts and lights. This was then blown up to A0 size for presentation to the client.

Artist: David Thody

Taken from a college project, these illustrations, below and opposite, show two narrow boats adapted for use as a travelling theatre. The artist drew the outline with a hard lead pencil and a steel rule, then scored it with a scalpel to prevent the marker colours from bleeding across it. He applied the basic background colours using Pantone Markers, and established the shadows by filling in with a light blue/grey. The pools of light on the stage were made by scoring with a scalpel, and then softening the area with coloured pencils. Section lines were picked out with a black, water-based ink Rotring pen.

10

Textiles

Marker is a medium well-suited to creating designs for textile printing. It can be used for bold designs with large areas of intense colour, and for smaller-scale patterns where the finer details are added in another medium, such as fineliner. Fabric printing techniques generally produce flat, ungradated colours, an effect which marker conveys well. And the free, rapid line of a marker drawing suits modern textile design perfectly.

All the designs shown in this chapter are for printed fabrics, rather than ones in which a pattern is woven into the fabric. This is because the nature of the weaving process excludes marker design. It is possible to weave complex patterns, or even tapestry pictures, on a programmed loom – in fact, the Jacquard loom of 1805 was the world's first programmable machine, reading the design from punched cards. This technique has been easily adapted to computer control, with the result that modern textile manufacturers design woven patterns directly on screen, cutting the graphic artist out of the process. However, fabrics with complex woven patterns are heavy and expensive, and printed fabrics are much more widely used.

The most common fabric printing method is a form of gravure printing using rollers engraved by a photographic process. For smaller runs, silk-screen printing is used, with either flat screens or hollow cylindrical ones which revolve like rollers. An old technique which is still in use is to print by hand with hand-engraved wood blocks. A modern method, increasingly used, is transfer printing, where the design is printed onto paper which is then applied to the fabric and heated, so that the colour vaporizes and transfers to the fabric.

One of the many concerns of textile designers is colour, and though many marker manufacturers offer big ranges the inability to mix means that they do not have the range or subtlety of paint. Even the complete ranges of several manufacturers would not offer the same choice as a box of paints. Nevertheless, this limitation seems to be more than compensated for by the clarity of the colours and the way that markers allow the artist to produce artwork which is a very good approximation of the final printed product.

Creating designs
Many designs for printed fabrics, especially those for clothes, are produced without any specific use in mind. That is the case with the designs by Gary Hinchliffe opposite and on page 142. Working from fashion forecasts, the artist simply draws a number of designs which are collected into a portfolio and shown to potential clients at trade fairs.

Obviously the designs are not produced completely at random. Different styles and sizes of pattern suit different fabrics and garments. The big, bold design on this page was created to suit a light cotton dress fabric – or, even better, silk, which would give extra intensity to the bright colours.

These designs are ordinary marker drawings on paper. No attempt is made at this stage to produce samples of printed fabric. It is quite likely that a client will want to buy a design but will ask for it to be modified in some way. For example, the colours might need to be changed to suit the prevailing shades of a garment house's coming collection. Or the client might prefer the design on this page without the French words, which might be unsuitable for certain markets.

Since the design is only a rapidly executed rough, it is simple enough for the artist to redraw it in a different colourway, or to make other changes.

Preparing for printing
When a design is printed, each colour is printed separately. It is therefore necessary to redraw the design completely, with each colour on a separate sheet. The very free and rapid execution of a style such as Gary Hinchliffe's is quite hard to recapture when making a series of tracings, particularly as all colours have to be traced in solid black so that they can be photographically reproduced.

Studio: Calver & Pound
Artist: Gary Hinchliffe

To produce this strident textile design, Magic Markers were applied directly onto cartridge paper – the artist choosing to start without any outline. This meant that his drawing had to be direct and confident. There was no room for indecision. He built up the design in patches of broad colour, and detail was added in black fineliner.

Studio: Calver & Pound
Artist: Gary Hinchliffe

The finer details of the design, above, were worked out initially in outline. Then the colour was blocked in with Magic Markers, and the details added with fineliner. Designs such as this are produced well in advance of season, and in a number of colourways. They are often modified later on – before printing the fabric.

Another Gary Hinchliffe design, below, drawn freehand without any outline. The profusion of colour and foliage was created with Magic Markers and a black fineliner. Outlines and coloured shapes were slightly offset, as if jostling for position, to reflect the lively tropical subject.

Pattern repeats

Most fabric patterns – except those used for single items such as headscarves – repeat. The larger design on this page was produced over an accurate pencil outline of the shape that will form the repeat. This shape does not have to be rectangular, but it must be exactly the same depth as, or an exact fraction of the depth of, the circumference of the printing roller of the machine, so that the roller can print a continuous line of repeats. Similarly it must be as wide as, or an exact fraction of the width of, the fabric (excluding the unprinted selvedge, or edge), so that two lengths of fabric can be joined neatly edge to edge with the pattern running smoothly over the join. If the pattern repeat forms an 'island', with no lines or shapes crossing its boundary onto the adjacent repeat, there is no problem as long as the shape of the repeat is accurately drawn. However, often patterns have continuous lines or shapes that run from one repeat into the next. Accuracy is needed to hide the join. This is particularly hard to achieve with free-flowing designs such as those of Gary Hinchliffe. For these it is preferable to plan to avoid any lines or shapes crossing boundaries.

Studio: Laura Ashley
Artist: Ian Brown

Below, the artist produced a detailed outline of the repeat in pencil, then coloured in a section with bullet-tipped felt pens.

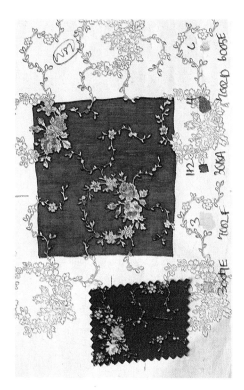

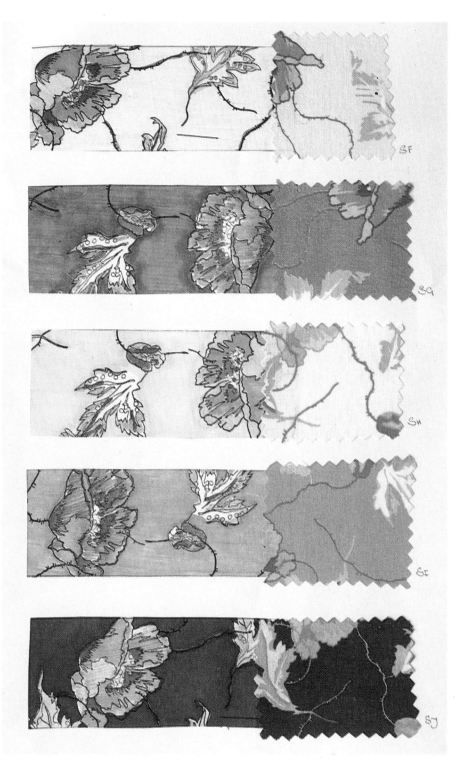

Designing to a brief

Not all designs are done 'on spec'. Laura Ashley fabrics are well-known for their small flower patterns, and the firm has its own design studio to create them. (Although the firm does produce other kinds of pattern, and is anxious not to get caught in a rut, popular demand forces them to keep producing similar designs.) Laura Ashley is best known for clothing, but also manufactures furnishing fabrics, wallpapers and other domestic items. Patterns are created in several colourways that can be combined with each other, or with plain fabric, paper or paint in one of the colours of the pattern. All this takes very careful planning, and the process is best suited to artists who are used to the house style. In this case, Ian Brown produced his sketches of different colourways by drawing an accurate pencil outline, copying it several times and colouring the copies. The fabric samples were made with a small silk-screen press, as a way of working out which colours should be used. Note the slight changes that have inevitably affected the design as the result of developing it from the original rough to a printed fabric. Most of the difference, however, is due to its being in a different medium on a different material.

For the design above five colourways were produced with felt-tipped pens, and presented alongside respective strike-offs on cloth. Both of these were used by the design co-ordination team to decide on the season's ranges.

Artist: Pat Albeck

The tea towel design, left, was one of a range of proposed products for the National Trust stall at Chelsea Flower Show. Stabilo series 68 felt tips were used to produce bright flamboyant designs which convey the ambience of the event. The white of the paper was skilfully utilized as a colour for the trellis, the daisies and the arum lilies.

A detailed rough, right, for a National Trust teatowel. The design was drawn with Pentel fibre tip on watercolour paper. Watercolour, gouache, fineliners and markers were used for colour and detail. This artist often uses brand new fine-tipped pens to produce quick but precise miniature visuals.

The visual below explores a herb theme, again for a range of National Trust products. It was produced on squared paper, mainly using green felt tips – as here, the artist often uses the French Baignol and Farjon marker range.

Product ranges

The National Trust is an organization with a clearly defined house style, but it does not have its own design studio. Instead, it employs artists like Pat Albeck, who designed everything on these two pages. The Trust's style even extends to a range of muted colours, such as the sage green which Pat Albeck refers to as 'National Trust green' (and for which she uses Pentel 132). By matching colours accurately she can produce a final printed textile which almost exactly replicates the artwork. Her teatowel designs, for example, are printed using five screens, so she uses five colours for her artwork and the dyes are matched to those. The Trust's small-scale, 'rustic' style calls for finely detailed line work, so these designs make extensive use of fine fibre-tipped pens.

One of the most interesting problems confronting a fabric designer is to design the decoration for a whole range of items in a similar style, using the same design motifs. The visual on the opposite page shows fabric items of different shapes – as well as various items of chinaware and tins. These are decorated with a motif of small sprigs of herbs. But note also how she has avoided monotony by introducing different, but related, themes into the range – herb names and a kitchen scene. She has also made good use of varied borders.

This textile design, 'Pansy', was produced for the John Lewis Group. Magic Markers were used to create the bold motifs that look as if they were made from collaged paper. A one-off design such as this would be produced to actual size, and in several colourways.

The image above was produced for a manufacturer of household items. A pencil outline was sketched in quickly, and rubbed down to prevent it breaking through the colours at a later stage. Most of the vegetation was done with Stabilo markers. Coloured felt tips, gouache and black fineliner were used to complete the picture.

11

Illustration

Most marker drawings are rough visuals never intended to be seen by the public. They are for use inside a studio, or at most for showing to clients. If a published picture is made on the basis of such a visual, it is usually in some other medium, and the marker original ends up in the waste paper bin. This is discouraging for marker artists. However, magazine and book illustrations are often done in marker, and reproduced directly from the marker drawings.

The range of illustrations

The illustrations on the following pages are highly varied, but they do no more than hint at the enormous range of types and styles of illustration work. Illustrators are required to provide everything from small diagrams in textbooks to entire picture books for young children, in which there may be no text at all. Styles vary from painstaking and minutely detailed realism to the broadest cartoons. A picture may be anything from a hasty black and white scrawl done in 30 seconds to an intricate multicoloured, mixed-media work that requires many preliminary sketches and takes several weeks to complete.

A good illustration can be much more than an accompaniment to a piece of text. This is most obvious in children's books, where the pictures may be more important than the words—and at the very least, the artist usually receives a credit the same size as that given to author. This is the case in other areas: romantic stories in women's magazines depend heavily on the mood created by the illustration on the opening page. This sets the tone for the whole dream world of the story, and gives the heroine and hero a recognizable face. Without this aid, the story may fail to convince the reader—or the reader might even refuse to begin reading a page of featureless grey text.

Setting a mood is even more important in book jacket illustration. The cover plays a large part in selling the book. To do this it must contain clues for the reader as to what the book is about. There are formal conventions governing these clues: pistols or bullets for thrillers, daggers for whodunits, embracing couples for romances and so on. The artist breaks these rules at his peril, for a book whose cover projects an unclear message will simply not be noticed by a potential buyer. (However, publishers have been known to break the conventions deliberately – for example, by putting a luridly sexy cover on a nineteenth-century classic. Provided that this ploy isn't overused, it probably sells quite a few copies to unsuspecting readers, who may be agreeably surprised by the text.)

Fashion illustration is a separate field, with its own styles and conventions. Fashion sketches may appear in magazines or be used inside the fashion trade. A range of examples are given on the following pages.

Another area of illustration which bridges several media is cartooning. The same artist may work for newspapers, magazines, books, television captions and commercials, and posters. The styles of well-known cartoonists are instantly recognized by the public, making them the most high-profile of all illustrators.

The need for a speciality

There is a huge and constant demand for illustration work of all kinds, but there are also vast numbers of illustrators looking for work. In order to get commissions, an illustrator has to make him or herself noticeable, so that when, say, a magazine designer wants a picture, the illustrator's name will come to mind at once. To be memorable, the artist needs a speciality: one narrow field in which he or she is supremely competent, so that when an illustration of that type is needed, he or she will be thought of first. An artist who is quite good in several fields is less likely to be successful, simply because that artist will be thought of second, and will only be commissioned if the first-choice artist has been too busy to take on the job.

Leading specialities include: figure work in various styles, from vaguely romantic to anatomically exact; food; technical illustration (not the same as design visualization—an example would be drawings for a car maintenance partwork); military hardware; science fiction subjects; pastiches of other styles, from old master paintings to 1950s adventure comics; and a huge variety of cartoon styles, from endearingly cosy to frankly horrible.

Illustrators will also specialize in certain drawing media, which are partly dictated by the style. For example, in order to get an adventure comic look, it is usually necessary to work in the same way as the originals were produced: pen drawings with three or four overlays for the crude, flat tints.

In fact, most illustrators can work in several styles, regardless of the speciality that gets them noticed in the first place. The illustrator will take his or her portfolio to whoever has commissioned him or her, and may frequently get a subsequent commission for work in one of his or her other styles. Often, illustrators are required to copy the style of an existing work. An example of this would be a book based on a television cartoon character, where the original animation studio was too busy to do the illustrations. Producing a plausible copy of someone else's style is uncommonly difficult, especially in a style that is so dependent on simple line drawing.

In contrast to this rather laborious work, illustrators often get commissions that are pure joy. Other commercial artists may have to work to a very narrow brief, but an illustrator can have a major say in the appearance of a complete book, choosing what he wants to illustrate and where he wants to put it—so that, for a change, it is the author who has to make his text fit the layout.

Illustration   147

Artist: Paul Davies

The cartoon pub scene, below, is one from
a series of 20 such illustrations,
representing scenes from 'typical' British
culture. The designer starts with a rough
pencil sketch and works the illustration up
by overlaying each stage. Pantone and
Magic Markers are used for the overall
background and major areas of colour.

The limits of technique

Robbie Veerman, an advertising artist who has only recently branched out into illustration, uses every possible technical aid to achieve the extremely fine detail in these pictures. These include a special Swedish bleedproof paper which is thin enough to lay over a preliminary sketch for tracing, and markers with interchangeable nibs so that he can draw much finer lines than with the standard chisel tip. Fineliner and crayons also contribute to the sharpness of the result.

When executing a drawing of this intricacy, it is necessary to plan very exactly the sequence in which the colours are applied in order to prevent pale colours from being sullied by picking up traces of darker ones already laid on the paper.

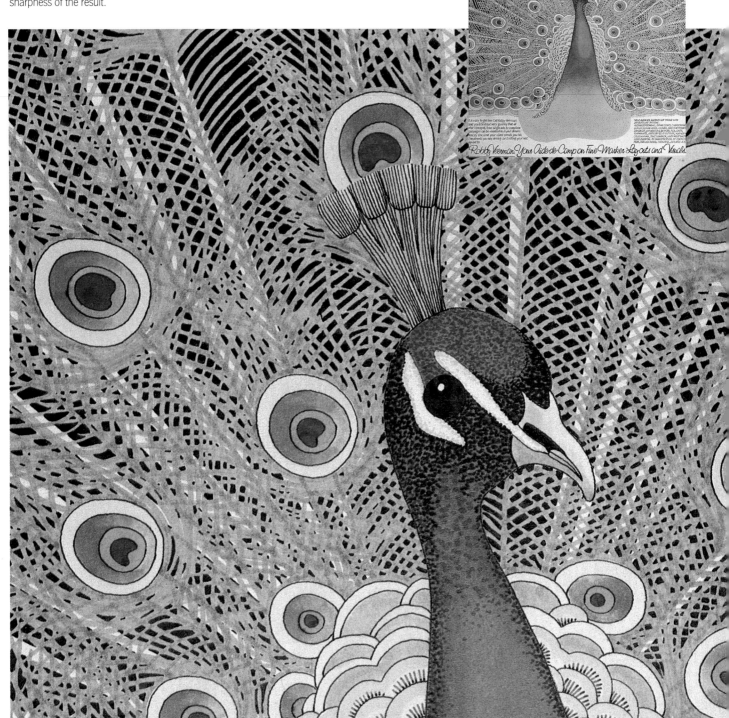

Illustration   149

Artist: Robbie Veerman

The illustration of a peacock, left, and detail below, was drawn initially in pencil. Then the outlines of all the white areas were traced off onto a separate sheet of marker paper. Placing the two sheets under a third, the artist filled in the colours, using Stabilo coloured pens, and slimgrip Pantone markers with interchangeable nibs.

To produce the bowl of fruit below Robbie Veerman followed the same procedure as for the peacock. To facilitate speed and accuracy, he worked from photographic references of the subject. Only Stabilo felt tip pens were used to establish the depth of colour on the fruit. The white paper provided the highlights, marker was used for the background, and white crayon was employed to 'texture' the fruit, and help add perspective.

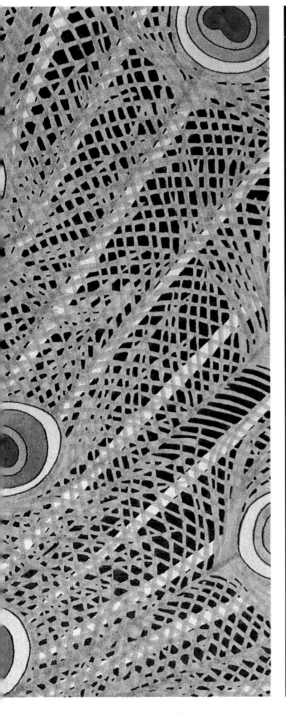

Fashion

Fashion illustration is very much a matter of presenting styles and images. Often, a carefully detailed and highly realistic picture of a model will fail to convey an accurate impression of the outfit she is wearing, whereas a brief sketch, to which marker is well suited, will succeed. There are a number of reasons for this. Firstly, clothes are rarely static. Because the wearer is constantly moving they swing and crease, and the light moves over them from various angles. So, the artist must capture that movement in his illustration. Secondly, too much attention to detail tends to detract from this sense of movement and, in some circumstances, can be simply irrelevant – for example, there is a marked tendency in fashion drawings for the model's legs to fade out below the hemline. Everyone knows she is wearing shoes of some kind, but there is no point in drawing them if the intention is to illustrate a dress. Thirdly, because fashion drawings are not intended to convey how a garment is made, details such as pocket flaps, for example, can be represented by just a simple curved line and a dot – instantly recognisable 'symbols' that will not clutter up the illustration. Finally, the sketchiness of fashion illustration is to some extent derived from the tradition of recording other peoples' designs at fashion shows – this has to be done very quickly, before the next model comes down the catwalk!

Artist: David Downton

Taken from the artist's portfolio, the illustration, left, is drawn with black Magic Marker. This facilitates a high-contrast, graphic approach to a fashion visual. The intention is to convey the general style of the garment, rather than the specific design.

Again, the intention of the illustration, above, is to present a high-contrast visual that conveys style, as opposed to a particular design. Here, black conté crayon is used for the figure drawing, black ink for the detailed work and Magic Marker and pastel for the colour – the essential purpose of the colour is to present the seasonal shades.

Illustration   151

This is a further example, left, of a high-contrast visual that conveys style. It was sketched in black Magic Marker, onto Hollingsworth paper. If the intention had been to present a specific design, then the illustration would have incorporated far more detail – such as buttons or belts – and the designer would have established the texture and weave of the fabrics.

This visual, above, illustrates another way of presenting a fashion image. In certain respects it is a more graphic picture than the others represented here – it is simplified and there is less line. In fact, it is similar to a screen print in the way that it presents a flat block of colour.

Illustration for children

There used to be two strongly opposed schools of thought about the style of illustration that was most successful for children's books. One was the 'keep it simple, keep it bright' faction, most strongly typified by Dick Bruna's books. These are for quite small children, but a comparable style has been used in many books for older children. The rationale for this style is to get the message across clearly. Though another, less obvious reason is that parents buy books, not children and parents with the no-frills, Bauhaus and Habitat tastes of the 1960s and 1970s would consider a lot of detail messy and irrelevant.

The other was the 'give them lots of detail' school, of which the most extreme example is the intricate street and factory scenes of Richard Scarry, with something going on in every corner. The idea is to stimulate the children by keeping their eyes and minds busy, and in fact anyone who has seen a child looking at one of these will know that it works.

However, there is now a third influence which is rapidly swamping the other two: the style of television cartoons. Many cartoon series have 'spin-off' books, which have to be illustrated in a style recognizably like that of the original. Television

cartoons have a grave defect: the high cost of animation means that all drawings have to be pared down to a few lines, filled in with flat colour (the shading and detail of the old Disney cartoons are a thing of the past). So, illustrators are forced to repeat this arid style.

The drawings on these pages are not television spin-offs. Though fairly simple, they have character. However, the animals in the drawing above are going to be transferred into a television cartoon series. Inevitably, much of the lively characterization and detail will be lost in the process.

Artist: Peter Kingston
Client: Macdonald Purnell

The illustration from a children's book, above, was produced by the artist who created the characters. Initially, he drew a pencil scamp, and then refined the picture by repeatedly tracing off the details with overlays. When satisfied with this stage, he finally traced off the illustration outlines onto marker paper, using black, water-based ink. To work up the final colour illustration he used a mixture of Pantone, Magic Markers and felt tip pens. (The Magic Markers are particularly useful in this sort of work, because they are flexible, and excellent for the purposes of reproduction.) This particular illustration took 2 hours to complete.

Illustration   153

Artist: John Astrop
Client: Macdonald Beehive

The illustrations above and left are from a series of children's books. The artist uses a storyboard method to develop the dialogue between the dog and the frog. He works on non-bleed paper and starts by drawing the outline. Then this is filled in with Pantone markers. Flat colour is used to give a cartoon-style effect.

Brushpen

Artists who are accustomed to working in marker take readily to brushpen. This is a fibre-tip pen with a tip almost as broad as that of a normal marker, but rounded rather than chisel-shaped, and considerably softer and more flexible. The thickness of the line it produces can be varied simply by altering the pressure on the point, so that very lively drawing is possible. The ink is water-based. After it has been applied to the paper it can be loosened and spread out with a brush moistened with plain water, giving gradations of colour in a much more controllable (and less smelly) way than by putting a solvent on marker lines. An effect akin to that of water colour can be achieved.

Brushpen can be used together with water-soluble coloured crayon, which can be spread in the same way. It can also be used with marker – a highly convenient arrangement because marker ink is not soluble in water, while brushpen ink is unaffected by lighter fuel and similar solvents. Thus either colour can be dissolved and spread over the paper independently of the other.

Artist: Christine Berrington

To produce the image right the artist used a mixture of media. She started with a pencil sketch on CS2 paper, then put a watercolour wash over it. She used Pantone marker for the basic form lines and flesh tones, then went over this with charcoal and pastel to achieve a textured tonal effect and convey the impression of movement.

For the illustration   left the artist used white cartridge paper. She sketched in the parrots with a combination of watercolour and Pantone markers. She put in the detail with Caran d'ache coloured pencils. The crayon was only partly wetted so that it added texture to the feathers.

Illustration   155

For the image left, on CS2 paper, Christine Berrington began by using blue marker for the background. However, the marker dried too quickly on the sky, so in the end she used a mixture of a watercolour wash and marker. Marker was used to put in the outlines, with pink Caran d'ache pencil on top to warm up the result. Pastel and charcoal were used to develop the tonal areas and shadows. Marker was used for the base skin tones, with Caran d'ache and pastel on top for tonal and shadow effects.

Artist: Martin Welch
Client: Over21 Magazine

Below: the artist xeroxed the actual products onto paper, then worked in colour with Edding brushpens, which lift the photocopier ink and diffuse the outlines. Next, he worked over them with Caran d'ache pencils to create the tones and highlights, and he used Pentel pens to add detail.

Index

Acknowledgements

The publishers would particularly like to thank Ralph Hancock, Judith More, Tom Porter, John Wainwright, Dick Ward and Laurence Wood – without their hard work this book could not have been produced.

Picture credits
The authors and publishers would like to thank the following individuals and organisations for their permission to reproduce the illustrations in this book:

Pat Albeck
4 Western Terrace
LONDON W6 9TX.

Brian Alldridge
Cymrick House
Station Road
Long Marston, Nr. Tring
Hertfordshire HP23 4QS.

Animation City
16–18 Beak Street
LONDON W1R 3HA.

Martin Asbury
Stonewold
Chapel Lane
Pitch Green
Bledlow, Nr Aylesbury HP17 9QG.

Laura Ashley
Carno
Powys SY17 5LQ.

John Astrop
Milton Court
Milton Street
Alfriston
Sussex BN26 5RJ.

Douglas Barber
Seymour Powell
2C Seagrave Road
LONDON SW6.

Christine Berrington
Meikeljohn Illustration
28 Shelton Street
LONDON WC2 H9HP.

Bellier Langford
56 Rosslyn Hill
LONDON NW3 1ND.

Harry Bloom
15 Melbourne Road
Teddington
Middlesex TW11 9QX.

Brennan Whalley Ltd.
131 Kingston Road
LONDON SW19 1LT.

Buz
43 & 45 Charlotte Street
LONDON W1P 1HA.

Paul Davies
6 Imperial Square
Cheltenham GL50 1QB.

The Design House
120 Parkway
LONDON NW1 7AN.

David Downton
24 Powis Square
Brighton BN1 3HG.

Drawers
8–10 Charing Cross Road
LONDON WC2 0HG.

Feref Associates
14–17 Wells Mews
LONDON W1A 1ET.

Trevor Goring
Helicopter Studios
28 Lexington Street
LONDON W1R 3HR.

Hop Studio
27–29 Central Buildings
24 Southwark Street
LONDON SE1 1TY.

Peter Kingston
Wimpole House
Trinity Street
Halstead
Essex CO9 1JQ.

Paul Langford
93 The Ridgeway
Cuffley
Hertfordshire EN6 4BG.

David Lee
13 Kensington Park Mews
LONDON W11 2EY.

David Leeming
Amerells
The Street
Little Clacton
Clacton CO16 9LX.

Leslie Millard Associates
7–8 Midford Place
LONDON W1P 9HJ.

Terry Lewis
8 Hill Gardens
Market Harborough
LEICS LE16 7PE.

L'Image
Watcombe Manor Farm
Ingham Lane
Watlington OX9 5EJ.

Jiricna Kerr Associates
7 Dering Street
LONDON W1R 9AB.

Lotus
Norwich
Norfolk NR14 8EZ.

The Michael Peters Group
11 Olaf Street
LONDON W11 4BE.

Carol Millard
Helicopter Studios
28 Lexington Street
LONDON W1R 3HR.

Claire Norbury
57 Hazelbourne Road
LONDON SW12 9NU.

Miranda Ottewill
18 Coventry Street
Brighton
Sussex BN1 5PQ.

PA Design
4A Princes Place
LONDON W11 4QA.

Gareth Pitman
80D Talbot Road
LONDON N6 4RA.

Presentation Design Consultants
5th Floor, Onslow House
60–66 Saffron Hill
LONDON EC1N 8QX.

Product First
10 Barley Mow Passage
LONDON W4 4PH.

Seymour Powell
2C Seagrave Road
LONDON SW6 2RP.

Storyboard Harpers
18 Greek Street
LONDON W1V 5LF.

David Thody
43 Tantataloon Road
LONDON SW12 8DF.

Robbie Veerman
60 Hartswood Road
LONDON W12 9NF

Martin Welch
Flat 5, 41 Colville Terrace
LONDON W11 2BX.

Wharmby Associates
35–37 William Road
LONDON NW1 3EK.

The following firms have generously provided
materials for photography:

Chartpak Ltd
14–17 Station Road
Didcot, Oxon.

Buffalo Pen and Stationery Co
15 Harbor Park Drive
Port Washington
NY 11050, USA.

DRG Royal Sovereign
100 Drayton Park
LONDON N5 1NA.

Frisk Products Ltd
4 Franthorne Way
Randlesdown Road
LONDON SE6.

Letraset VK Ltd
195–203 Waterloo Road
LONDON SE1 8XJ.

Meccanorma Ltd
10 School Road
LONDON NW10

Staedler Ltd
Ponyclun
Mid Glamorgan
Wales.

Schwan Stabilo Ltd
74 Buckingham Avenue
Slough, Berks.

Every effort has been made to trace the copyright
holders and obtain permission to reproduce the
illustrations in this book, we apologise in advance
for any unintentional omissions and would be
pleased to insert the appropriate acknowledgement
in any subsequent edition of this publication.

The publishers would also like to thank Ken
Greenley and the students of the Transport Design
Department at the Royal College of Art, London and
the Michael Peters Group for their invaluable help
and kind co-operation during the making of this
book.

The illustration on page 86 is reproduced by
permission of Arthur Shepherd.

Special photography: Ian Howes and Nadia
Mackenzie.